MARIA MITCHELL

MARIA MITCHELL

The Soul of an Astronomer

Beatrice Gormley

William B. Eerdmans Publishing Company
Grand Rapids, Michigan

© 1995 Wm. B. Eerdmans Publishing Co.
255 Jefferson Ave. S.E., Grand Rapids, Michigan 49503
All rights reserved

Printed in the United States of America

00 99 98 97 96 95   7 6 5 4 3 2 1

Library of Congress Cataloging-in-Publication Data

Gormley, Beatrice.
Maria Mitchell: the soul of an astronomer / Beatrice Gormley.
          p.   cm.
Includes bibliographical references and index.
Summary: A biography of the first female science professor at Vassar
College and the first American woman astronomer.
ISBN 0-8028-5116-9 (cloth: alk. paper). —
ISBN 0-8028-5099-5 (paper: alk. paper)
1. Mitchell, Maria, 1818-1889 — Juvenile literature. 2. Women
astronomers — United States — Biography — Juvenile literature.
[1. Mitchell, Maria, 1818-1889. 2. Astronomers.
3. Women — Biography.]   I. Title.
QB36.M7G67   1995
520'.92 — dc20
          [B]   95-21980
                                                CIP
                                                AC

The author and publisher gratefully acknowledge permission to quote
material from the sources listed on page 118.

To my husband, Bob,
for his unfailing support and encouragement —
and for that initial connection

Contents

Introduction

O ne evening in the autumn of 1847, a young woman left the party going on in her house and climbed up to the observatory on the rooftop. She wasn't the only one scanning the skies that night; in all the observatories of Europe and America, the most competitive astronomers were hoping to find a new comet. A prize, a gold medal, had been offered for such a discovery. But it was this young woman, Maria Mitchell, who put her eye to her telescope and spotted the new point of light with a fuzz around it, just above the North Star.

Maria's discovery of Comet Mitchell, or 1847 VI, won her the coveted gold medal and made her famous. But as heavenly bodies go, a comet is not a fitting symbol for Maria Mitchell. Halley's comet, for instance, appears only once every seventy-six years. It rushes toward the sun from the dark, outer reaches of the solar system, makes a blaze across our sky for a few weeks, and then disappears into the dark again.

Maria Mitchell is more like a star of the first magnitude, because she radiated a steady brilliance throughout her lifetime and long afterward. In a time when most women were not even allowed to study advanced mathematics, she became an accomplished astronomer before she was thirty. Later, as the first professor of astronomy at Vassar College, she used her worldwide reputation to promote the causes of women's rights and women's education.

Astronomy, as Maria Mitchell taught it, was a means for training her students to think independently. "Until women throw off this reverence for authority," she wrote, "they will not develop." But "when they come to truth through their investigations, when doubt leads them to discovery, the truth which they get will be theirs."

All her life, Maria Mitchell pursued her own truth. Studying the truth that science offered, she felt in touch with the Creator of the universe. "Every formula which expresses a law of nature," she wrote, "is a hymn of praise to God." She was continually inspired by her work, watching the stars far into the night. As she wrote in her diary, "There is the same enjoyment in a night upon the housetop, with the stars, as in the midst of other grand scenery; there is the same subdued quiet and grateful seriousness; a calm to the troubled spirit, and a hope to the desponding."

At the same time, she was baffled by the presence of evil in the world, and by her own painful experience of the death of people she loved. With typical honesty and persistence, she did not stop asking disturbing questions, nor did she accept answers she did not truly believe.

Still, Maria's friends were struck by her "deeply religious nature," as a teacher at Vassar put it. Maria "had no sympathy with free thinking — so called — or scientific speculations, flippant and irreverent." In a diary entry for New Year's Day, 1855, she recorded her thoughts about God as the ideal friend: "A friend is not to be found in the world, such as one can conceive of, such as one needs, for no human being unites so many of the attributes of God, as we feel our nature requires, in one who shall be guide, counsellor, well-wisher & the like."

Maria Mitchell's nonconforming and honest habit of mind was unforgettable to the people who knew her. "Her freedom from all the shams and self-deceptions made an impression that elevated my whole standard, mental and moral," wrote one former student. "Far more interesting than anything Miss Mitchell ever did," added another student, "was Miss Mitchell herself."

Here is the path-breaking woman scientist, the inspiring teacher, the quirky, playful friend, the earnest seeker after truth. Here is Maria Mitchell herself.

CHAPTER 1

A Devout Astronomer

On August 1, 1818, in the "birthing room" off the kitchen of a gray-shingled house in Nantucket, a baby girl was born to William and Lydia Mitchell. She was their third child, and they named her Maria (Ma-RYE-ah).

Later, the whole world would find out that Maria Mitchell was born with extraordinary gifts. But according to her sister Phebe (whose collection of Maria's letters and journals is the best source about her early life), "as a little girl, Maria was not a brilliant scholar; she was shy and slow." Maria herself remembered as a milestone one day in "dreary dark December" when she went to school to meet a new teacher. Her feet were cold, and her heart was pounding with fear, but the teacher calmed her down and began to teach her "the love of books." Long afterward, Maria described this teacher who "first made the lesson book charming" as one of the "three persons who made epochs in my life."

1

As Maria grew older, her talents emerged — all the qualities for the making of an astronomer. For one thing, her vision, including her perception of color, was unusually keen. In addition, she could measure very precisely, and she had a strong sense of the relationships between objects in space. If she came into a room and a chair was out of place, she would line it up exactly parallel to the wall.

Maria was also patient and persistent, willing to work for hours to solve a problem or understand a concept. And she had a gift for mathematics, which is the basis for astronomy. Still, if Maria Mitchell had been born in any other place or to any other family, it is unlikely that she would have become an astronomer.

First of all, Maria was lucky enough to be born into the unique community of Nantucket. For almost a hundred years, the people of this small island off the coast of Massachusetts had depended on whaling for their livelihood. From their little "elbow of sand," as the author of *Moby Dick* would describe the island, Nantucketers sailed out into the Atlantic and Pacific and Indian Oceans in pursuit of whales and their highly prized oil. Before the development of petroleum products, the people of Europe and America depended on whale oil to light their homes and cities and to lubricate machinery. Nantucket might have lacked good farmland and timber and hunting, but it had grown into the foremost whaling port in the world.

There were two distinct parts to the town of Nantucket. The waterfront was a bustling international port, noisy and colorful and smelly. The businesses of craftsmen who supported the whaling ships crowded the wharves: sail makers, rope makers, barrel makers. There were inns for the seamen, who might be Portuguese or black or even South Sea Islanders, as well as Nantucket men of English stock. Over all hung a knockout stench from the whale-oil refineries and warehouses. Maria's older brother, Andrew, would be lured into this world, shipping out on a whaler when he was a young teenager.

Whaling brought wealth to Nantucket, but it was hard and dangerous work. The crews of the whalers had to stay at sea for years, and sometimes they met with disaster and didn't return. Meanwhile, the women at home had to run the family store or the farm, as well as the household, without male support or supervision. This must have been a lonely life, but it gave Nantucket women the independence, and the chance to prove their abilities, that most nineteenth-century women lacked.

Up the low hill from the harbor was the other part of Nantucket: a Quaker village. In this part of town, the people dressed in sober black and gray and brown and lived clean, quiet, orderly lives. Many of these people looked alike for the good reason that they were related. The Starbucks and the Macys and the Barneys and the Folgers and the Colemans and the Mitchells had all lived on Nantucket for generations, marrying each other and raising big families. When Maria was older and had moved away from the area, someone mentioned to her that she had met a cousin of hers on Nantucket. Maria retorted, "Oh, very likely. I have five thousand cousins there."

Compared with other groups of the time, Quakers were democratic and respectful of women. In the seventeenth century, it was the enterprising and forceful Mary Starbuck who had made Quakerism the main faith on Nantucket. Kezia Coffin of the eighteenth century became a wealthy merchant — although the Friends later disowned her for dressing fashionably and for buying a spinet for her daughter. In Maria's time, women as well as men were elders in the Society of Friends, and women as well as men preached during First Day (Sunday) meeting.

The other piece of unusual luck for Maria was her father. William Mitchell loved astronomy, and he loved to teach. When the Mitchell children were young, he was not very good at making money; although he invested once or twice in a whaling expedition, his bets didn't pay off. In an attempt to support his large family, he worked at a number of different jobs, including farming, refining whale oil, and building barrels for the oil. But whatever he was doing for a living, he was also observing the heavens every clear night. And in one way or another he was always teaching.

William Mitchell gave lectures on astronomy to learned societies; he invited his neighbors to look at the moon through the telescope in his backyard. When Maria was four, he opened a small school for young children, which he ran for a few years, until Nantucket decided to provide public education. Then Mr. Mitchell taught in a public school for a few years, but he disliked the large classes and the need to keep discipline. He quit to start a "select" school of his own, to be run according to his ideas about education.

William Mitchell's ideas about education were most unusual for the time. "Punishment of any kind was almost unknown," he wrote of his school. "We met together as common friends and for mutual improvement." Maria herself, as well as at least one of her sisters, attended this school. Unfortunately, Mr. Mitchell couldn't make his school pay, and finally he closed it and went to work for a bank.

Still, he couldn't help but teach. His favorite subject was astronomy, and his favorite pupils were his own children. Although Maria and her much younger brother Henry were the only ones who showed a clear talent for astronomy, the Mitchell children were all indoctrinated by their father.

The person Mr. Mitchell most admired was William Herschel, the English astronomer who had discovered the seventh planet, Uranus. Herschel had also constructed his own telescope, the most powerful of his era for studying faint, distant objects, and he had catalogued hundreds of double stars and galactic nebulae. His far-reaching (although not always correct) theories on the distances of the stars, the nature of the Milky Way, and the structure of the universe itself were a stimulus to other astronomers. Maria's sister Phebe claimed that if anyone had asked one of the Mitchell children the question "Who was the greatest man that ever lived?" the child would have answered without hesitating, "Herschel."

As each Mitchell child became old enough, Mr. Mitchell would have him or her assist with his observations of the stars and other heavenly objects. This was not just a hobby — astronomy had a very practical use in nineteenth-century Nantucket. The captains of the whaling fleet used precise records and predictions of the movements of stars and other heavenly bodies to help navigate their ships. One of William Mitchell's side businesses (which included acting as a justice of the peace and an executor of wills) was correcting ships' chronometers, the extremely accurate clocks needed to determine a ship's position on the seas.

Some of the Mitchell children thought it was merely tedious to stay up past bedtime and watch the stars inch along overhead to the ticking of a chronometer. But Maria loved it. Quickly she grasped the mathematical principles behind the movements of the heavenly bodies and learned to make the complicated calculations.

Maria loved working alone with her father, and she loved spending hours under the sparkling splendor of the night sky. Just as the whaling ships of Nantucket sailed out from their tiny island to the farthest parts of the globe, so Maria and her father launched themselves, with their eyes and minds, to the moon and the planets and the outer reaches of the universe.

One of William Mitchell's favorite mottoes was "An undevout astronomer is mad." How could you raise your eyes to the night sky and not be filled with awe? How could you study the solar system and the stars and not see the universe as evidence of a mighty Creator?

In this area of her spiritual life, Maria always agreed with her father. She memorized a poem by Joseph Addison that expresses the same idea:

The spacious firmament on high,
With all the blue ethereal sky,
And spangled heavens, a shining frame,
Their great Original proclaim.

All her life, whenever Maria was frightened or distressed, she recited this poem to herself, and it always calmed her.

❂   ❂   ❂

In February of 1831, Maria was twelve and a half. The town newspaper, the *Nantucket Inquirer,* reported great excitement about the coming solar eclipse. (A solar eclipse occurs when the moon comes between the earth and the sun.) Nantucket was in an excellent position for viewing this particular eclipse, and William Mitchell had been looking forward to it for years. In 1829 he

7

had drawn up a set of calculations, predicting the path of the eclipse as well as when it would occur and how long it would last, for his astronomy class. This was to be an *annular* (ring-shaped) eclipse. In a *total* eclipse, the moon appears to be the same size as the sun and blacks out the entire disk of the sun. But during an annular eclipse, the moon appears to be smaller than the sun and is circled by a thin ring of fiery light, the outer edge of the sun.

As a passionate astronomer, William Mitchell would have watched the eclipse in any case. But charting its course would also give him a chance to determine the exact longitude of his gray-shingled house on Vestal Street. This would allow him to correct ships' chronometers even more precisely.

The day of the eclipse, February 19, was icy but clear. Since it was too cold to spend the three hours of the eclipse outside, Mr. Mitchell lifted out one of the windows in his parlor and set up the telescope in front of the open frame. Maria held the chronometer on her lap and counted off the seconds. Her father watched the eclipse through the telescope, his eyes shielded by a special kind of dark glass.

Together, Maria and her father recorded the exact split second that the shadow of the moon touched the rim of the sun, the instant that the shadow formed a ring inside the sun, and the instant that the ring was broken. Maria, not yet thirteen, was well on her way to becoming her father's partner in his lifetime passion.

❂   ❂   ❂

William Mitchell, according to his brother Peleg, never had any desire to go to sea. He was too much of a homebody. In 1820, when he was elected a member of the commission to revise the Massachusetts constitution and had to spend six weeks in Boston, he missed his family terribly. If Maria thought about it, she must have been thankful that her father was unlike the many Nantucket fathers who spent years at sea on whaling voyages.

However, Mr. Mitchell did have to be away from home now and then on business. In his absence, Maria began to correct ships' chronometers on her own. It is interesting to imagine what a weather-beaten whaling captain thought of turning over his precious chronometer to this young girl in a gray Quaker dress and white cap. His ship's very safety depended on the chronometer, for a chronometer only one second off would cause a ship to be a quarter mile off course. Could William Mitchell's young daughter make the necessary observations of the stars with the sextant (an instrument with a small telescope for measuring the altitudes of celestial bodies), and perform the computations absolutely correctly afterward?

Maybe her mother vouched for Maria's ability — Lydia Mitchell was known to be almost painfully honest. Mr. and Mrs. Mitchell were always struggling to feed and clothe their large family, and the chronometer earnings must have been welcome. But Lydia Mitchell, as her husband described her, would not have told a lie to save a child's life, much less to get the fee for "rating" a chronometer.

Lydia Coleman Mitchell was the parent who ran the household. Mr. Mitchell was so kindly and indulgent that he had a hard time getting the family horse to behave. Left to himself, William Mitchell would have given his children anything they asked for. But his wife kept discipline and managed the family budget. She also considered carefully how each child should be educated, according to his or her special abilities, and prepared to earn a living. Running this household was a major — and long-lasting — undertaking, because over time the Mitchells had ten children, born about two years apart: Andrew, Sally, Maria, Anne, Frank, William Forster, Phebe, the twins Henry and Eliza (Eliza died at the age of three), and Kate.

Mrs. Mitchell had been a librarian before her marriage, and now, although she no longer had time to read herself, she directed her children's reading. The Mitchells read novels and stories and poems, and of course the Bible and religious books such as the *Journal* of George Fox, the founder of the Quakers. They also read the *Nantucket Inquirer*, which, besides reporting on Nantucket affairs, included articles about the latest scientific advances and news from all over the world.

Living in a community of thrifty, hard-working Quakers and being brought up by a thrifty, hard-working mother, Maria was as industrious as any of them. Like the other girls, she learned to sew her own clothes, to cook family meals in the kitchen fireplace, and to keep the house neat. "If she swept a room," said her sister Phebe with understatement, "it became clean."

As one of two older girls in a family of ten, Maria was expected to look after the younger children. Luckily she enjoyed taking care of them and entertaining them, and they enjoyed her. Although Maria would never have children of her own, all her life she would make friends with nieces and nephews and friends' children. Among her papers, along with her astronomical records and college lecture notes, are stories and poems she wrote for her young friends and letters she exchanged with them.

By the time she was fourteen, Maria had learned most of what her father had to teach her about mathematics. He knew well that advanced mathematics was the key to astronomy, and he always regretted that he had not gone further in this study himself. Encouraging Maria to develop her obvious talents, the Mitchells sent her to Cyrus Peirce's new school "for young ladies" in Nantucket.

Like William Mitchell, the Reverend Peirce was a dedicated teacher. Unlike Maria's father, however, he was impatient and demanding. Still, he recognized Maria's unusual talent and eagerness to learn. Under Peirce's guidance, she soon progressed to such advanced mathematics-related subjects as conic sections (the study of the various possible intersections of a cone with a plane) and the principles of navigation.

At home, Maria was allowed a place of her own for studying. This was significant, because space was precious in the little gray house, with its few small bedrooms for as many as eleven people. The Mitchell children usually did their lessons sitting around the table after supper. But now Maria was given a study at the bottom of the garret stairs. It was the size of a small closet, just big enough for what she needed: a few shelves, one of which served as a desktop; a chair; a whale-oil lamp; and her books and papers. And — most important of all — privacy.

CHAPTER 2

A Quaker Family

The Mitchells, who were members in good standing in the Nantucket Society of Friends, went to meeting every First Day. (The Friends called Sunday "First Day," Monday "Second Day," and so on, refusing to name the days of the week after pagan gods.) They sat for hours on the hard wooden benches of the meetinghouse: Mr. Mitchell, Andrew, Frank, William Forster, and later little Henry on the men's side; Mrs. Mitchell, Sally, Maria, Anne, Phebe, and eventually Kate, the youngest, on the women's side. (Eliza, since she died so young, may never have been brought to meeting.) There was no reading from the Bible, no sermon, and no hymn-singing or music of any kind. The windows of the meetinghouse were plain glass, and there were no pictures or statues. The idea of the meeting was to wait on God in silence, without any distractions.

The poet John Greenleaf Whittier, a deeply religious Quaker who later became a good friend of Maria and her father, expressed his experience of the Friends' meeting in his poem "First-Day Thoughts":

There, syllabled by silence, let me hear
The still small voice which reached the prophet's ear.

One of Maria's younger brothers, William Forster, who remained a Quaker all his life, later described the sensation of silent worship: it was like watching the waves break on the shore, he said. In fact, he remembered a deeply felt moment of watching the surf on the Nantucket shore with his father. "Just think, my son," said William Sr. reverently. "Ever since the foundation of the world."

What did young Maria think about during the long hours of meeting? Maybe she watched the squares of sunlight from the windows, gliding over the black hats and gray bonnets and white caps of the gathered Friends. Maybe she silently recited lines from her favorite poem, "The spacious firmament on high," to accompany the slow progress of the sunlight:

The unwearied sun from day to day
Does his Creator's power display;
And publishes to every land
The work of an almighty hand.

Toward the end of the meeting, someone might feel moved by the Spirit to speak. That person would stand up, take his hat or her bonnet off, and say whatever words came. Finally, one of the elders, sitting on the "facing bench" in the front of the bare room, would end the meeting by shaking hands with the man next to him.

Like many of the other families on Nantucket, the Mitchells and the Colemans (Maria's mother's family) had belonged to the Society of Friends, or Quakers, for generations. One of their ancestors, Peter Folger, had been among the first settlers of Nantucket. He had come to the island in the 1600s to escape being punished by the New England Puritans for giving shelter to Quakers in a storm.

When the Society of Friends was still a small, persecuted sect, it had focused on the inner person and the Divine Light that shone in each soul. The Friends' plain dress and speech and their bare and silent meetinghouses were only means to an end. They were meant to help people ignore worldly concerns and concentrate on their relationship to God.

But by the time Maria Mitchell was growing up, the Friends of the Nantucket Meeting were no longer the persecuted ones — they were the ones in control of the island's government and business. In fact, many Friends had done very well in the whaling business. They had become so prosperous that they now had to work at proving they were not worldly, and so they grew more and more concerned with following the set of rules that the Friends called the Discipline.

There were so many rules to follow: *Don't wear bright*

colors or fashionable clothes. Always address another with "thee" and "thou." Go to meeting every First Day. Don't play music — don't even sing or hum. Don't put any markers on graves. Don't marry a non-Quaker. Don't fall asleep in meeting. And so on.

If a Friend broke too many rules, he or she would be spoken to by an elder. And if the rule-breaker did not repent, he or she could be "read out" of Meeting — expelled. In a small, tightly knit community like Nantucket, the members of the Meeting were all relatives, neighbors, and probably business associates. Accordingly, being exiled from the group was a serious matter.

Lydia Mitchell, a dignified, self-controlled woman, followed the Quaker rules carefully. William Mitchell was more apt to bend the rules he thought were unreasonable, although he didn't take his religion lightly by any means. All his life he attended meeting faithfully, not because it was the rule but because, as he wrote in his memoirs, "few persons have better enjoyed the silent meetings of Friends."

William Mitchell dressed plainly, but he filled his house and yard with color. He tended to choose books with red covers for his bookshelves, and he painted the stand for his telescope a brilliant red. The walls of the sitting room in the house on Vestal Street were papered with pink roses, while a glass ball hanging from the ceiling flashed rainbows around the room. The back garden was bright with real roses and other flowers.

The Mitchell children, too, felt free to bend some

rules. The girls learned how to sew by practicing on dolls' clothes, but they didn't sew plain little gray dresses for them. "There was a great delight in gratifying the fancy," Maria's sister Phebe recalled, "in dressing the dolls . . . in all of the most brilliant colors and stylish shapes worn by the ultra-fashionable." No one seems to have scolded them for it.

On First Days, even after meeting, Friends were supposed to spend their time in a quiet, serious way. But here, too, the Mitchells were lenient with their children. Anne, two years younger than Maria, remembered one Sunday afternoon when she and Andrew (who had not yet run away to sea) were allowed to escape to the garret.

On this particular day, the rest of the family had gathered in the sitting room. The baby was sleeping in his cradle, Mr. Mitchell was napping in his chair, and Maria was absorbed in a book. Children were not supposed to play games on Sunday, and they were allowed to read only books on religious subjects or, in the practical Nantucket spirit, textbooks. So Anne and Andrew each carried a schoolbook up the two flights of stairs to the garret. But the two of them understood that their parents mainly wanted them to be quiet.

The garret was a storage place — for the dried fish and herbs hanging from the rafters, and also for the visual aids that their father used in his lectures on astronomy. There were white sheets with diagrams of the solar system sewn onto them, and hardwood balls half a foot and more in diameter, which represented the various planets. The day before, Andrew had constructed a "steamboat" in the garret, using a board painted with the motto "AN UNDEVOUT ASTRONOMER IS MAD" for a mast, and one of the sheets for an awning. He used the wooden balls to weight down the corners of the "awning."

Anne and Andrew were silently but happily playing "steamboat" when a draft in the garret tugged the sheet enough to move one of the "planets." It rolled against another planet, which in turn knocked into another. To the children's horror (but maybe also delight), the entire wooden solar system bumped and rumbled down the stairs from the garret to the first landing, and from the landing down into the sitting room, coming to rest at their father's feet. Later in life, Anne joked that perhaps it was this incident that first sparked Maria's interest in astronomy.

❂   ❂   ❂

The reasoning behind the Friends' quiet and sober way of living was that this life was not important in itself. Our life on earth, they believed, was a preparation for life after death. And the question was, *Where* were you prepared to go after death — to heaven or to hell?

The Puritan influence was strong in New England, among the Quakers as well as the Methodists, Baptists, and other sects. Most people of that time saw nothing wrong with frightening children into good behavior, but Maria's parents seem too gentle and kind to have terrified their children with stories of eternal punishment. However, Maria certainly read some such tracts, perhaps given out by the Friends concerned with religious education. One story that particularly stuck in her mind was titled "Never-too-late-to-mend," featuring a "Black Hole" of punishment for those who *didn't* mend.

Quakers (as well as other Christians of that time) also thought it was good for young people to hear inspirational stories about dying children. The saintly boys and girls in these stories didn't mind dying, because they were sure they were going to heaven. As they were leaving this life, they preached sermons to their parents.

Maybe Maria thought of these stories when Eliza, her youngest sister and Henry's twin, fell sick and died at the age of three. Maria was the older sister who spent so much time with the younger children. "She was a capital story-teller," according to her sister Phebe, "and always had a story on hand to divert a wayward child, or to soothe the little sister who was lying awake, and afraid of the dark." Maria was also a good nurse. But there was nothing her stories or care could do for little Eliza.

In the nineteenth century, many children died young of diseases that are easily cured or prevented today: diphtheria, polio, measles, whooping cough, tuberculosis, pneumonia. In fact, compared with other families of the era, the Mitchells were fortunate because out of their ten children, only one died in childhood. But this good fortune would have been no comfort to Maria as she left the meetinghouse and followed the procession of Friends with Eliza's little coffin. In the hummocky, grassy graveyard at the end of Vestal Street, Eliza was buried in an unmarked grave, as was the Quaker custom.

What sense did Maria make of her baby sister's death? It couldn't have been anything like the happy deaths in those pious tracts. Maybe this was the beginning of the questions of faith that nagged at Maria Mitchell, off and on, all of her life. For her, the biggest question was whether she would rejoin the people she loved after death. Sometimes this was easy for her to believe; sometimes it was not. She longed to know for sure.

In 1853, when she was an adult, Maria wrote of a dear cousin who had recently died, "I could not help thinking of Esther a few evenings since when I was observing. A meteor flashed upon me suddenly, very bright, very short-lived; it seemed to me that it was sent for me especially, for it greeted me almost the first instant I looked up, and was gone in a second — it was as fleeting and as beautiful as the smile upon Esther's face the last time I saw her. I thought when I talked with her about death that, though she could not come to me visibly, she might be able to influence my feelings;

but it cannot be, for my faith has been weaker than ever since she died, and my fears have been greater."

Because of her doubts about the faith of her ancestors, Maria privately wondered, growing up, if she was destined for hell. Years afterward she asked a friend in surprise, "And did you never lie awake in terror of Hell? . . . When I was a girl of sixteen, I often did, afraid of being a lost soul forever. Such was the doctrine I heard preached in my childhood!"

Some Quakers, including Maria's parents, her brother William Forster, and the poet John Greenleaf Whittier, were able to ignore such terrifying doctrines. For them, being a Quaker meant peace and inspiration and a deep sense of the Divine Light within, guiding their lives. But Maria was too honest with herself and others — the very quality that made her a good scientist. She could not simply accept the parts of Quakerism she liked and ignore the parts she hated. Later, this unswerving honesty would cause her trouble more than once.

CHAPTER 3

A Temple of Knowledge

A hard worker all her life, Maria was proud that she was able to earn her own living. By the time she was sixteen, she was no longer a student but a teacher of mathematics at the school run by the Reverend Cyrus Peirce. The following summer, she helped her father survey the island of Nantucket for a new map. Then she opened a grammar school of her own. And only a year after that, at the age of eighteen, she was offered the ideal job.

A library society had recently bought the former Universalist church on Pearl Street, an imposing building reminiscent of a white-pillared Greek temple. The society incorporated itself as the Nantucket Atheneum. The Atheneum would be not only a library housing their collection of 3,200 books, but also a cultural center. A roomy lecture hall was constructed on the second floor, and a museum room was set aside for a collection of curiosities from the South Seas. The well-to-do Nantucketers who established the Atheneum respected books and knowledge. They were proud to put the money they had made in the whaling business into their temple of knowledge.

In the fall of 1836, the Nantucket Atheneum was ready to open to the public. Like other libraries of the time, the Atheneum was not free, but one could become a shareholder for a small donation. Even financially struggling families like the Mitchells could afford to belong.

When the proprietors of the Atheneum offered the job of librarian to Maria, she accepted; they paid her sixty dollars a year to start. Being a former librarian herself, Lydia Mitchell must have been happy for her daughter. Mrs. Mitchell had been an avid reader, devouring all the books in both the libraries where she had worked. After her marriage, the unrelenting labor of running a large household had left her no time for reading, but once her children were grown, she eagerly took up the practice again. Much later, after her death, her husband even thought she had brought on her final illness by staying up reading in the cold.

For Maria, the schedule of the Atheneum was perfect. The library was open every weekday afternoon and on Saturday evening. That meant that Maria could do her share of the housework at home early each day. Then she could spend the rest of the morning in the Atheneum, reading and studying and working the computations for her astronomical observations. And most of her evenings would be free for telescope work.

Like her mother, Maria was a voracious reader, and to her the Atheneum offered a feast. She read novels, including those by Sir Walter Scott and James Fenimore Cooper, and poetry and plays, including the works of Shakespeare. In addition, she read all kinds of scientific books and journals. Since many of them were written in Latin or German, she taught herself those languages so that she could read even more. It was at the Atheneum that she found, read, and digested Pierre-Simon de Laplace's *Celestial Mechanics,* a massive five-volume work detailing the relationship of every member of the solar system to every other member.

Maria was not so unusual in this regard; self-education was a tradition among her relatives. Her own father had taught himself mathematics and astronomy. In the Folger branch of the family, there was self-educated Benjamin Franklin, whose mother was a Nantucket Folger. A closer relative was an eccentric cousin, Walter Folger, Jr. This odd but brilliant man accomplished such feats as building from scratch — constructing each part himself — a clock that displayed the tides and the movements of the sun and moon. Then there was another cousin, the mathematically talented Phebe Folger, who "taught navigation to her husband," according to Maria, "and he became, in consequence, the captain of a ship."

In effect, Maria's access to the Atheneum allowed her to give herself a college education. And it was a good thing that Maria Mitchell was capable of educating herself, because the doors of the best colleges in the country were closed to her. The only college that admitted women as well as men was Oberlin College in Ohio, established in 1833.

However, at that time astronomy in America was so backward that even Harvard College could not have given Maria a better education than she received at home. The Harvard Observatory was not even established until 1839, when the College invited expert clockmaker and astronomer William Bond to move his telescope and other equipment from his private parlor in Dorchester to Cambridge. There Bond served without pay as the official Harvard astronomer. It was not until 1847 that Harvard was able to purchase and mount in an observatory dome a fifteen-inch telescope, as large as any in the world.

Furthermore, Maria had the chance to associate with first-rate thinkers in the Mitchells' own parlor. William Mitchell was a highly respected amateur scientist. (Most scientists were amateurs at that time.) He was acquainted with many distinguished American scientists, including William C. Bond.

Given Maria's studies at the Atheneum, her discussions with the prominent scientists who visited Nantucket, and her unlimited use of her father's astronomical equipment, she probably received as good an education at home as she could have at Harvard or Yale.

The Nantucketers who used the Atheneum library were also part of Maria Mitchell's education. "Her visitors in the afternoon were elderly gentlemen of leisure," wrote Phebe, "who enjoyed talking with so bright a girl on their favorite hobbies. When they talked Miss Mitchell closed her book and took up her knitting, for she was never idle."

There were young visitors to the Atheneum too, many of whom took Maria as their mentor. She was always glad to recommend books and discuss their reading, and they responded to her friendly interest by confiding their problems and dreams. "A young sailor boy came to see me to-day," she wrote in her diary entry for April 18, 1855. "It pleases me to have these lads seek me on their return from their first voyage, and tell me how much they have learned about navigation. They always say, with pride, 'I can take a lunar [observe the moon's position with a sextant to determine a ship's position], Miss Mitchell, and work it up!'"

One of Maria's young assistants at the library, Alexander Starbuck, grew up to write a history of Nantucket. He remembered his delight at being invited to come by Maria's observatory and look at the moon through her telescope. All his life he kept a complimentary letter she wrote to him after he had left the Atheneum.

Lilla Barnard, another of Maria's young friends, told years later how timid she had felt by herself in the cavernous Atheneum, and how the kind librarian "always had a few moments to chat." Lilla, too, was thrilled to be invited to Maria's observatory, to look at the planet Venus.

The Lyceum, a series of public lectures and entertainment hosted by the library, made the Nantucket Atheneum a cultural center for New England as well as the island. Distinguished visitors of all kinds came to speak in the Atheneum's upstairs hall: philosopher Ralph Waldo Emerson, writer Henry David Thoreau, Unitarian minister and reformer Theodore Parker, naturalist Louis Agassiz, ornithologist and artist John James Audubon, abolitionist and women's rights advocate Lucy Stone, newspaper editor Horace Greeley, poet John Greenleaf Whittier. In 1841, an anti-slavery convention was held in the same lecture hall. Urged on by the fiery abolitionist William Lloyd Garrison, ex-slave Frederick Douglass gave his first public speech to an enthusiastic audience.

Now that she had a salary, Maria began saving for a trip to Europe. This had been a dream of hers since she was a child. Growing up in a town where most of the men went off on long, exotic trips, she itched to see the world for herself. And her reading had connected her with the culture of Europe. In the mid-1800s, the United States was still a young, rough country, and Americans looked to Europe as the source of real civilization — the fount of the arts, history, science. A trip to Europe was supposed to be the crowning touch to a really good education.

Maria knew it would be years before she could save enough money to visit Europe, but she had plenty of patience and self-control. "She dressed very simply,"

27

wrote Phebe, "and spent as little as possible on herself
— which was also true of her later years."

About the same time that Maria Mitchell became the
librarian of the Atheneum, William Mitchell was appointed cashier of the Pacific Bank. At last he was
assured a decent salary to support his family. And at
last the Mitchells would have roomy living quarters.
One of the benefits of William's new job included the
use of the spacious apartments in the Pacific Bank building, a handsome brick structure at the top of Main
Street.

The bank building was stable enough that Maria and
her father were able to set up a little observatory on the
rooftop. William Bond, who would be appointed director of the Harvard Observatory in a few years, and who
had constructed an impressive private observatory in
his own house, came from Boston to Nantucket to help.
The equipment that William Mitchell already owned
was supplemented by the instruments lent to him by
the U.S. Coast Survey; included was a fine four-inch
telescope. The arrangement was mutually beneficial:
Maria and her father would do work for the Coast
Survey and have the use of the telescope for their own
observations.

At this time Nantucket had a lively social life, and
the other Mitchell girls, in spite of being Quakers, often
went out or entertained at home. But Maria "cared but
little for general society," noted Phebe, "and had always
to be coaxed to go into company." Every clear night,

Maria put on her "regimentals," as she called the hood, coat, mittens, and boots she wore to protect her from the cold, and climbed up through the attic to the rooftop observatory. She preferred the company of the stars.

Maria must have been a woman of unusual energy, to work all day and then most of many nights without exhausting herself. She described a day — a day on which she filled in for an absent servant girl, but did *not* watch the stars — in her diary:

I was up before six, made the fire in the kitchen, and made coffee. Then I set the table in the dining-room, and made the fire there. Toasted bread and trimmed lamps. Rang the breakfast bell at seven. After breakfast, made my bed, and "put up" my room. Then I came down to the Atheneum and looked over my comet computations till noon. Before dinner I did some tatting, and made seven button-holes for K. [probably her youngest sister, Kate]. I dressed and then dined. Came back again to the Atheneum at 1:30, and looked over another set of computations, which took me until four o'clock. I was pretty tired by that time, and rested by reading *Cosmos* [an important scientific work by Alexander von Humboldt]. Lizzie E. came in, and I gossiped for half an hour. I went home to tea, and that over, I made a loaf of bread. Then I went up to my room and read through (partly writing) two exercises in German, which took me thirty-five minutes.

It was stormy, and I had no observing to do, so I

sat down to my tatting. Lizzie E. came in and I took a new lesson in tatting, so as to make the pearl-edged. I made about half a yard during the evening. At a little after nine I went home with Lizzie, and carried a letter to the post-office. I had kept steadily at work for sixteen hours when I went to bed.

❂   ❂   ❂

One night during the dry July of 1846, the Mitchells woke up to the urgent clanging of the church bells. A fire had begun on Main Street and was sweeping through the town. The townspeople, including the Mitchells, hurried out to fight the fire. But the town had no fire department, and the fire-fighting efforts were confused. It seemed that the Pacific Bank building, at the top of Main Street, and the wooden Methodist church next to it, would go up in flames soon.

But the winds blew the fire in another direction, and the church was spared. The brick bank building did not burn, either, although the wooden observatory shed on the Mitchells' rooftop did catch on fire. In spite of the Mitchells' efforts, their instruments and records were damaged.

For Nantucket, the fire was a terrible calamity. After the smoke cleared, the townspeople saw that a third of Nantucket, mainly the business district, had gone up in flames. The waterfront, with its highly flammable whale-oil warehouses, was completely destroyed.

In a different way, the Great Fire of 1846, as it came to be called, was a disaster for the historical record about Maria Mitchell. Maria, fearing that her personal papers might get scattered around if the bank building caught fire, burned her diaries and letters herself.

One of the worst losses to Nantucket was the Atheneum, which burned to the ground with all its books and other treasures. This must have seemed a terrible blow at first, but with surprising swiftness the proprietors raised money and built a new Atheneum. It looked even more like a graceful Greek temple of knowledge than the first building had. Maria sent out a plea for books, and libraries and schools and individuals all over the country donated almost 1,800 volumes.

Just six months after the fire, the new Atheneum library opened for business again. In May of 1847, Ralph Waldo Emerson came to Nantucket to help dedicate the new building. And the lecture series began again.

The Mitchells rebuilt their rooftop observatory, and Maria and her father went back to their nightly sky-watching and record-keeping. The following year, Maria would see a different kind of fire over Nantucket — a light in the sky that would change her life.

CHAPTER 4

No Longer a Friend

Long before the Great Fire of 1846, Maria Mitchell had begun to have doubts about her membership in the Society of Friends. Since she destroyed her diaries from the early 1840s, we have no record of her thoughts at this time. Perhaps she was increasingly disturbed by the hypocrisy of certain Friends, important members of the Meeting. Quakers were supposedly dedicated to the good of the community, but they had resisted the establishment of a free public-school system on Nantucket. They held that slavery in the South was an "anti-Christian practice," but they treated the seamen on their own profitable whaling ships little better than a plantation owner treated his field hands.

All her life, Maria Mitchell scorned pretense of any kind. Several years after the fire, at a point when she was discouraged about her life and achievements, she consoled herself in her diary that at least "I have not pretended to what I was not." Genuineness was an important value to her, and it was a quality in her that other people always noticed. A photograph of Maria taken in the 1840s shows her looking directly at the camera with large, dark, thoughtful eyes. It is a gaze that would make any hypocrite uncomfortable.

Unlike her sisters Anne and Phebe and Kate, Maria didn't mind the Quaker rules about clothing and lively parties and music. Maria didn't want to wear fashionable clothes in bright colors; all her life she wore plain, sober clothing. Maria didn't care much for socializing, either; she would rather go up to the rooftop by herself and watch the stars. And Maria didn't want to sing and play the piano. In fact, she had no ear for music at all. She used to send her younger brothers and sisters into delighted gales of laughter by croaking out a song.

However, most of the Mitchell family, including Mr. and Mrs. Mitchell, enjoyed music. In spite of the Quaker rule against it, Mr. Mitchell had always encouraged his children to sing. But knowing that Friends had been disowned by the Meeting for keeping a piano, he would not go so far as to buy one himself.

But when all the Mitchell daughters (even tone-deaf Maria contributed money) plotted to buy a piano themselves and bring it into the house, they must have been confident that Father wouldn't mind. In fact, Mr. Mitchell was openly glad on the day he came home to hear piano chords sounding from the upstairs parlor. "Play something lively!" he urged.

Soon the news of the piano in William Mitchell's

house reached the elders of the meeting, and a sober-faced old Friend came to question him. Putting on a serious face himself, Mr. Mitchell explained that it was not *his* piano; it was his daughters'. And he thought it best, if they were going to enjoy music, for them to do so at home. Besides, Mr. Mitchell pointed out with a twist of reverse logic, he was the Society's agent, responsible for the property of the Meeting. Did it not reflect badly on the Society for its accredited agent to be "under dealings," as they called this kind of investigation?

The fact that the Friends accepted William Mitchell's excuses for the forbidden piano in his house showed how much the strict Quaker influence on Nantucket had waned. Seeing the Mitchell girls get away with it, "several other young Quaker girls eagerly seized the occasion to gratify their musical longings," Phebe noted.

Maria's problems with the Friends, however, would not be solved by getting away with breaking a rule or two. She wasn't sure she believed what they believed, and she couldn't pretend. Her mind naturally took the scientific approach, in which belief came only after objective examination and proof. Someone else's say-so, even that of the entire Society of Friends, did not constitute proof. The farthest Maria could go, as she wrote later in her diary, was to say to herself, "There is a God and He is good. . . . I try to increase my trust in this, my only article of creed."

If Maria did not believe, she could not pretend. Like

her mother, she was almost painfully honest. In later years a friend at Vassar College, Frances Wood, remembered Mr. Mitchell's joking comment: "If thee has any secrets, thee mustn't tell them to Maria. She never could keep one." He didn't mean that she would betray a confidence, but that she simply said what was on her mind. "Thought and word with her came pretty close together," said another friend.

If the truth reflected poorly on Maria, she felt especially obligated to tell it. During her early years at Vassar College, she sent some astronomical observations to the Coast Survey that were returned as not accurate enough. Maria promptly informed the president of Vassar, John Raymond, although otherwise he wouldn't have known anything about it. Maria explained in her letter,

> I would not have troubled you with all this, but as I have probably said to you that I was as good an observer as there was in the country (which I believed) I wish to take it back.
>
> Yours, meaning to grow humble,
>
> M.M.

Independence of mind was also important to Maria, not only as a scientist but as a self-respecting person. She deeply resented anyone else telling her what to believe. Years later, she heard a preacher say, "The unbeliever is already condemned." She responded in her diary, "It seems to me that if anything would make me an infidel, it would be the threats lavished against unbelief."

For Maria, perhaps the most troublesome questions of faith were about death. In March of 1842 a little nephew, her sister Sally's boy, died of a paralysis. This apparently cruel and senseless death may have been on her mind when she stopped attending meeting.

The next year, Maria went to meeting one last time. Then she was visited by two women, a delegation from the Nantucket Meeting of the Society of Friends. They reported back to the Meeting that Maria Mitchell "informed us that her mind was not settled on religious subjects, and that she had no wish to retain her right in membership." Shortly afterward, Maria was formally disowned by the Nantucket Meeting. She was twenty-five.

Maria's parents must have been sorry to see her turn away from the faith of generations of Mitchells and Colemans, the faith of so many relatives and neighbors. Although Mr. and Mrs. Mitchell didn't agree with the Meeting in everything, "they believed it best to conform to the rules of Friends," as Phebe explained. But evidently they did not expect to control their grown children's decisions about religion; just the month before, Maria's brother Andrew had been disowned by the Meeting for marrying a non-Quaker. And Mr. Mitchell had his own difficulties with the more conservative Quakers. Two years after Maria's disowning, Mr.

Mitchell and some like-minded Friends split off to form their own, more liberal Nantucket Meeting.

Maria Mitchell herself never joined another church, although she regularly attended the Unitarian Church on Nantucket. "Her sympathies, as long as she lived, were with that denomination, especially with the more liberally inclined portion," wrote Phebe. But in many ways Maria remained Quaker-like. She continued to dress in plain, sober-hued clothes. In fact, years later, students at Vassar noted "the Quaker-like garments which she daily wore." They also noted her Quaker-like disdain for titles. It was a mark of favor for Professor Mitchell to call a student by her last name, without the customary "Miss."

Within her family, Maria always used the Quaker "plain speech." Her brother William Forster, who remained a devout Quaker, commented dryly that to Maria the Friends' way of talking was only a kind of family heirloom, a sentimental keepsake. But Maria's heritage from the Friends went much deeper than sentimentality. Qualities about her that struck people many years later — her simplicity and directness, her scrupulous honesty with herself and others — had been encouraged by her Nantucket Quaker upbringing.

Maria also admired the moral courage and independence of mind that were more essentially Quaker-like than the Friends' drab clothes and "plain" speech. After all, the Society of Friends had originally been started by men and women determined to follow their inner

Divine Light, even if they were jailed or hanged for it. Quakers were pacifists, although being against war usually meant that both sides regarded the Quakers as the enemy. The War of 1812, for instance, had almost ruined the prosperous economy of Nantucket.

Quakers were also among the most zealous abolitionists. The Nantucket Friends had come out against slavery before the American Revolution. The "President of the Underground Railroad," Levi Coffin of Indiana, was a Friend of Nantucket heritage. In 1841, the first of three anti-slavery conventions was held in Nantucket. The poet John Greenleaf Whittier, who was a devout Quaker, first became known for his anti-slavery poems. Lucretia Coffin Mott, a distant cousin of Maria's, became famous — infamous, many thought — working for abolition and for women's rights. Another cousin, Anna Gardner, was also an ardent fighter for abolition and women's rights.

Maria longed to know what she should do with *her* life. Study the stars, of course — but she seemed to feel that her life had a purpose beyond her passion and talent for astronomy. A few years later she would write in her diary, "To know what one ought to do is certainly the hardest thing in life. 'Doing' is comparatively easy."

CHAPTER 5

Comet Mitchell

In the mid-nineteenth century, new developments in astronomy were expanding the field at an exciting rate. The distances of the nearer stars had recently been calculated. The existence of "dark" companion stars to Sirius in Canis Major and Procyon in Canis Minor, two of the nearest stars, had been deduced. Many expected Vulcan, a theoretical planet presumed to be even closer to the Sun than Mercury, to be spotted any day.

Neptune, the eighth planet, actually had been first sighted in 1846 by the German J. G. Galle. Maria happened to be visiting the Harvard Observatory shortly after the discovery of Neptune was announced. By this time, the director of the observatory, William Bond, and his son George had become good friends of the Mitchells through their mutual passion for astronomy. They wrote frequent letters and exchanged visits, discussing astronomical ideas and techniques and observations. The very night of Maria's arrival at Harvard,

Professor Bond identified Neptune, which looked like a small star, because it was in a different position than it had been in the night before. Maria was thrilled to get a look at Neptune through the Harvard Observatory telescope, knowing she was one of the first people in America to see the eighth planet.

Only a few years before, the sun-grazing comet of 1843, so bright that it was visible in broad daylight, had heightened public interest in comets. Like everyone interested in astronomy, the Mitchells and the Bonds were aware that the King of Denmark awarded a gold medal to anyone who discovered a "telescopic" comet — one too faint to be seen with the naked eye. No American had won this medal yet, although George Bond had actually discovered a telescopic comet. But he had lost his chance for the medal because he had not complied with the rules of the competition. The possibility of winning this prize may have been in the back of Maria's mind as she swept the sky with her telescope every clear night. "No matter how many guests there might be in the parlor," wrote Phebe, "Miss Mitchell would slip out, don her regimentals as she called them, and, lantern in hand, mount to the roof."

Devoted as Maria was to astronomical work, it was often painstaking, tedious, and even maddening. In December of 1854 she recorded the following description of trying to track a comet. It shows how important her patience and hard work, as well as her talent, were to her success:

A host of little annoyances crowded upon me. I had a good star near it [the comet] in the field of my comet-seeker, but *what* star?

On that rested everything, and I could not be sure even from the catalogue, for the comet and the star were so much in the twilight that I could get no good neighboring stars. . . .

Then came a waxing moon, and we waxed weary in trying to trace the fainter and fainter comet in the mists of twilight and the glare of moonlight.

Next I broke a screw of my instrument, and found that no screw of that description could be bought in the town. . . . However, the screw was made, and it fitted nicely. The clouds cleared, and we were likely to have a good night. I put up my instrument, but scarcely had the screw-driver touched the new screw than out it flew from its socket, rolled along the floor of the "walk," [and] dropped quietly through a crack into the gutter of the house-roof. I heard it click, and felt very much like using language unbecoming to a woman's mouth.

I put my eye down to the crack, but could not see it. There was but one thing to be done, — the floor-boards must come up. I got a hatchet, but could do nothing. I called father; he brought a crowbar and pried up the boards, then crawled under it and found the screw. I took good care not to lose it a second time.

The instrument was fairly mounted when the clouds mounted to keep it company, and the comet and I again parted.

41

❂   ❂   ❂

On the night of October 1, 1847, a little over a year after the Great Fire, Maria left the party going on at the Mitchells' and climbed up to the rooftop observatory as usual. She put her eye to the four-inch telescope, the high-quality instrument that the U.S. Coast Survey had lent to the Mitchells. A short while later, Maria spotted a new object, something that looked like a fuzzy star, just above the North Star. A nebula (a mass of interstellar dust or gas) might look like that, but there was no nebula in that particular place in the sky. Maria was sure of that — she knew the stars of the Northern Hemisphere as well as she knew the streets of Nantucket.

So the "fuzzy star" must be a comet, still too far from the sun to have a tail (which is created by solar photons pushing the cloud of dust particles around the comet away from the sun). Maria hurried to get her father, and he agreed with her. "This evening at half past ten," William Mitchell wrote in his diary that night, "*Maria discovered a telescopic comet five degrees above Polaris.*" He urged his daughter to announce her discovery. But unassuming Maria could not believe that she, rather than one of the distinguished astronomers of Europe, had first spotted the comet.

That did seem unlikely. Nevertheless, William Mitchell wrote to William Bond at the Harvard Observatory. He asked Bond to drop Maria a note to let her know whether the comet had been seen by his son George, who was sweeping the skies as industriously as Maria, or by anyone else.

George Bond wrote Maria a teasing letter:

> Dear Maria: There! I think that is a very amiable beginning, considering the way in which I have been treated by you! If you are going to find any more comets, can you not wait till they are announced by the proper authorities? At least, don't kidnap another such as this last was.
>
> If my object were to make you fear and tremble, I should tell you that on the evening of the 30th I was sweeping within a few degrees of your prize.

Unfortunately for Maria, by the time William Mitchell's letter reached William Bond, Father de Vico at the Vatican Observatory in Rome had already announced his discovery of the same comet on October 3. The rules for awarding the gold medal stated that the discovery must be announced immediately, and so it seemed that Maria had lost her chance for this prize. But when Professor Bond told the president of Harvard College, Edward Everett, about Maria's discovery, he began a campaign to get Maria her just reward.

Everett wrote to the German scientific journal *Astronomische Nachrichten,* explaining the special circumstances. George Biddell Airy, astronomer at the Royal Observatory in Greenwich, England, replied to

Everett that they couldn't bend the rules for Miss Mitchell. However, the King of Denmark could do so if he wished.

President Everett then wrote to R. P. Fleniken, an American diplomat in Copenhagen, explaining the whole situation and asking for help in the name of "all the friends of science in America." Fleniken obligingly conveyed to the King of Denmark, in flowery diplomatic language, the whole history of Maria Mitchell's discovery of the comet, along with copies of the documenting letters. On October 6, 1848, a year and five days after Maria had put her eye to her telescope and spotted the new comet, an answer came from the palace. The King of Denmark had indeed decided to award the prize to Miss Maria Mitchell of Nantucket. At the age of thirty, Maria had won an international honor.

President Everett, to whom the medal was sent, was elated over this triumph for American science. Maria was the first American, as well as the first woman, to win the medal. Everett opened the box and gloated over the medal a bit, showing it off to the Bonds and to Benjamin Peirce, professor of mathematics and the leading mathematician in the country, before sending it on to Maria. On one side of the medal a motto in Latin was stamped into the heavy gold: *Not in vain do we watch the setting and rising of the stars.* Below it was the date that Maria, before anyone else in the world, had seen the comet. Around the edge of the medal, in capital letters, was printed MARIA MITCHELL.

❂   ❂   ❂

Now Maria was a celebrity. In some ways this was unpleasant for her. She was shy and unpretentious, and she thought much of the fuss was ridiculous. Visitors began to come to the Atheneum just to stare at the "lady astronomer." In 1855 she mentioned one of them, a "Western gentleman," in her diary. "I wish I could swop half my head for half yours," he had told her.

Visiting Boston a few years after she received the medal, Maria noted dryly, "It is really amusing to find one's self lionized in a city where one has visited quietly for years; to see the doors of fashionable mansions open wide to receive you, which never opened before. I suspect that the whole corps of science laughs in its sleeves at the farce."

When the artist Hermione Dassel came from New York in 1851 to paint Maria's portrait, the story is that Maria urged her youngest sister, Kate, to pose with their father instead. Certainly the graceful young woman in that double portrait, wearing a pink-skirted dress, with a velvet ribbon at her bare throat and rings on her fingers, holding a chronometer, is not Maria. Maria herself finally did sit for a portrait, looking into her telescope, wearing a Quaker-like black dress with a modest white-lace collar. The intent gaze of the large, dark eyes and the set of the determined chin are unmistakably hers. In this picture, it is clear that what Maria looks *like* is not important compared with what she is looking *at*.

In spite of all the nonsense of celebrityhood, Maria found some genuine advantages to being a world-famous astronomer. In 1848, she was inducted into the American Academy of Arts and Sciences. She was the first woman to be so honored, and it would be almost a century before another woman was recognized by the Academy. Maria was delighted at the chance to associate with her colleagues and especially to learn the latest in scientific circles firsthand. She attended meetings of the Academy with her father, who, as a highly respected amateur astronomer, had been a fellow (the Academy was unsure about calling Miss Mitchell a "fellow") since 1842.

Joseph Henry, a well-known physicist and the director of the newly established Smithsonian Institution in Washington, D.C., also wanted to recognize Maria's achievement. He sent her a grant of one hundred dollars, which moved her deeply. Perhaps at this point she began to sense her unusual position in society, and the unusual power to do good that came with it.

Maria's status as a respected astronomer also gave her new opportunities for employment. In 1849 Charles Davis, the superintendent of the new *American Ephemeris and Nautical Almanac*, invited her to work as a computer for this ambitious government project. Maria's assignment (a bit sexist) was to compute the tables predicting the daily position of the planet Venus, named after the Roman goddess of love.

Still, it was an honor to be employed by the *Almanac*

along with other noted American astronomers and Professor Benjamin Peirce of Harvard. She was now the first professional woman astronomer in America. Maria was also pleased with the salary: three hundred dollars per year in addition to her salary at the Atheneum. Her dream of visiting Europe, the continent of Herschel and Shakespeare and Newton and Sir Walter Scott and Galileo, was beginning to look like a real possibility.

CHAPTER 6

The Hardest Year

M aria Mitchell never married. Why not? One answer is that she was not conventionally pretty.
She was tall and bony, and her voice was deep. Also,
she was dark-skinned in a time when extreme fairness
was admired. Later in life she casually referred to herself
as ugly, although her friends would not have agreed. A
former student at Vassar denied indignantly that she
"would have changed her [Miss Mitchell's] face with its
dark, grand eyes . . . for the pretty features of the reg-
ulation type, such as you may see any day."

As a young person, Maria was also rather shy in
social gatherings. She may have been glad she had a
good excuse to avoid parties by going to the rooftop to
work with her telescope. One journalist, describing
Maria shortly after her death, speculated that she had
turned to astronomy because Nantucket was so quiet
and isolated. But this was not the case. When Maria

was young, Nantucket had a lively social life, and she had to make an effort *not* to take part in it.

Of course, many plain, shy people do get married. There has been speculation that George Bond, Maria's young astronomer friend and rival, may have been in love with her. But there is no evidence that Maria ever wanted to marry him or anyone else.

When Maria was professor of astronomy at Vassar, an article about her was published, hinting that her early hopes for romance had been blighted. In a letter to a friend, Maria called the article a "mixture of truth and falsehood." She added, "I have seen my family laughing over it. What a pity that no 'blighted affections' can come into the story of my life! It would pay a newspaper so much better!"

Maybe the reason Maria Mitchell never married was simply that she didn't want to end up like her mother. Maria adored her father, as did most people who knew kind, gentle William Mitchell. But it must have been clear that Maria's mother was the one who had given her entire life over to the family. In a gossipy letter to a young woman friend, Maria mentioned another friend who had broken off a romance with a Dr. Clark. "She said he was selfish — is any man not?" Although Lydia Mitchell was an energetic, disciplined person, running a household and caring for ten children had consumed her. Maria may have seen marriage as a trap that would lock her into a lifetime of "women's work."

In a diary entry she made in 1853, Maria reacted angrily to Dr. Hall, an author who thought that women should spend even more time sewing than they already did. "It seems to me that the needle is the chain of woman, and has fettered her more than the laws of the country," she retorted. ". . . I would as soon put a girl alone into a closet to meditate as give her only the society of her needle. . . . Suppose every man should feel it is his duty to do his own mechanical work of all kinds, would society be benefited? would the work be well done? Yet a woman is expected to know how to do all kinds of sewing, all kinds of cooking, all kinds of any *woman's* work, and the consequence is that life is passed in learning these only, while the universe of truth beyond remains unentered."

So Maria may have deliberately chosen to put her own energy and discipline into her passion — astronomy. In that field of the "universe of truth," discoveries continued to open up the cosmos to human understanding. Methods of measuring the actual brightness of a star were invented. At Harvard, the Bonds began to use that new technique, photography, to capture the moon and then the stars. The German scientist Alexander von Humboldt publicized Samuel Schwabe's discovery that sunspots (which would become a special interest of Maria's) occurred in about eleven-year cycles.

The first several years after her discovery of the comet were full ones for Maria. There were her routine astronomical observations, which gave her more than routine pleasure. "I 'swept' last night two hours, by three periods," she noted in her diary on March 2, 1854. "It was a grand night — not a breath of air, not a fringe of a cloud, all clear, all beautiful. I really enjoy that kind of work, but my back soon becomes tired, long before the cold chills me. I saw two nebulae in Leo with which I was not familiar, and that repaid me for the time. I am always the better for open-air breathing."

There was also Maria's continuing work at the Atheneum, and trips to Boston and New York to attend meetings and buy books for the library. On one of these trips Maria met Dorothea Dix, the reformer who was improving the way mentally ill people were treated. Maria greatly admired this woman's work, but she was chilled by her manner. "In her general sympathy for suffering humanity, Miss Dix seems neglectful of the individual interest," Maria wrote in her diary. ". . . It is sad to see a woman sacrificing the ties of the affections even to do good. I have no doubt Miss Dix does much good, but a woman needs a home and the love of other women at least, if she lives without that of man."

Maria's home was still the spacious apartments of the Pacific Bank building. Her older brother and sister were married and gone, but there were still six Mitchells at home besides Maria and her father and mother. In addition to this large family, Maria had close friendships with other women. In December of 1854 she mused in her diary, "The love of one's own sex is precious, for it is neither provoked by vanity nor retained by flattery;

it is genuine and sincere. I am grateful that I have had much of this in my life."

By this time, however, Maria was beginning to feel dissatisfied. She was thirty-six years old. Her work at the Atheneum, so ideal eighteen years ago, now seemed boring and irritating. "I have determined not to spend so much time at the Atheneum another season," she wrote at the end of the summer of 1854. A week or two later, going over her computations for a new comet she had observed, she noted, "I have had a fit of despondency in consequence of being obliged to renounce my own observations as too rough for use. The best that can be said of my life so far is that it has been industrious, and the best that can be said of me is that I have not pretended to what I was not."

There was a "despondency" about the town of Nantucket, too. Even before the Great Fire of 1846, the whaling industry on Nantucket had been dwindling. Now, although most of the business district of the town was rebuilt, the waterfront industries that supported the whaling fleet were not, because there was little need for them. The center of whaling had moved to New Bedford, on the mainland.

The population of Nantucket had also dwindled as many, especially the ambitious young people, left the island to find work elsewhere. In 1849, the Gold Rush in California had lured even more people away from Nantucket.

But a sadder phase of Maria's life was about to start.

Maria discovered "Comet Mitchell" when she was only twenty-nine. This portrait, painted shortly after her discovery, shows a woman intent on her work. Photo of comet by members of the Lunar and Planetary Laboratory team of the Catalina Observatory, January 15, 1974; courtesy of NASA. Painting of Maria Mitchell by Hermione Dassel, 1851; courtesy of the Nantucket Maria Mitchell Association.

Nantucket harbor in winter. The snow and cold and ice would sometimes "lock up" the harbor and bring the town to a virtual standstill. Courtesy of the Nantucket Historical Association

(*Above*) The Mitchell family home on Vestal Street in Nantucket: the birthplace of Maria Mitchell.
Courtesy of the Nantucket Maria Mitchell Association

(*Left*) The Mitchell family home in the Pacific Bank Building, where William Mitchell worked as cashier. Courtesy of the Nantucket Historical Association

Maria with her sisters. (She stands on the left
in the back row.) Even as a young girl, Maria
showed a special interest in astronomy.
Courtesy of the Nantucket Maria Mitchell Association

(Left) John Greenleaf Whittier, the poet and Friend who wrote about the experience of Quaker worship in his poem "First Day Thoughts." Courtesy of the Friends Historical Library of Swarthmore College

(Below) The interior of the Nantucket (Wilburite) Friends Meetinghouse. It was kept plain so that worshipers could concentrate on God. Courtesy of the Friends Historical Library of Swarthmore College

(Right) William Bond, one of the prominent scientists who visited Nantucket and became friends with Maria and her father.
Courtesy of Harvard University Archives

(Below) The Nantucket Atheneum. Maria's job as librarian here gave her time to study the stars at night.
Courtesy of the Nantucket Historical Association

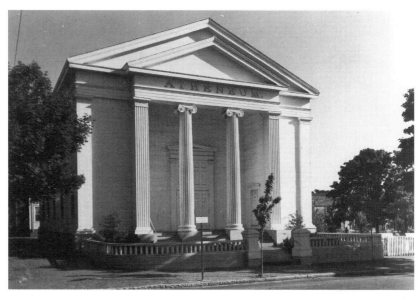

Shortly after Maria discovered Comet Mitchell, Hermione Dassel
came to Nantucket to paint Maria's portrait. Although she
eventually persuaded Maria to sit for her, Maria was
initially resistant to the idea. She urged her father
and her sister Kate to pose for this portrait instead.

View of Nantucket, ca. 1805, by Thomas Birch. When Maria
was thirty-eight, she was finally able to sail out of this harbor
en route to Europe. She took with her letters of introduction
to the top astronomers on the continent.

Courtesy of the Nantucket Historical Association

(Left) Matthew Vassar, the founder of Vassar College, asked Maria to serve as Professor of Astronomy and Director of the Observatory at the college. Photo by Slee Brothers, Poughkeepsie, NY; courtesy of Special Collections, Vassar College Libraries

(Below) A view of Vassar College Main Building, from an engraving by John A. Powell, ca. 1860s. Courtesy of Special Collections, Vassar College Libraries

Maria with her class in front of the observatory, ca. 1878.
"We especially need imagination in science," she told her
students. "It is not all mathematics, nor all logic, but
it is somewhat beauty and poetry."
Courtesy of Special Collections, Vassar College Libraries

Maria with her students on the steps to the dome, 1885.
As the picture suggests, Maria and her father had their
living quarters in the observatory building.
Photo by Vail Brothers, Poughkeepsie, NY;
courtesy of Special Collections, Vassar College Libraries

Not surprisingly, Maria gave her students ample exposure to the women's movement. Maria was friends with many of the influential women of her time, and she invited them to Vassar. Among the guests were writer Louisa May Alcott (*top l.*), suffragist Lucy Stone (*bottom l.*),

suffragist Elizabeth Cady Stanton *(top r.)*, and writer and reformer Julia Ward Howe *(bottom r.)*.

(*Above*) Maria with her father, William. He loved the stimulating atmosphere at Vassar. Unfortunately, he died in 1869, only a few years after Maria had accepted her position there. Photo by Slee Brothers, Poughkeepsie, NY; courtesy of Special Collections, Vassar College Libraries

(*Right*) Frances Wood, a fellow teacher and good friend of Maria's at Vassar. Courtesy of Special Collections, Vassar College Libraries

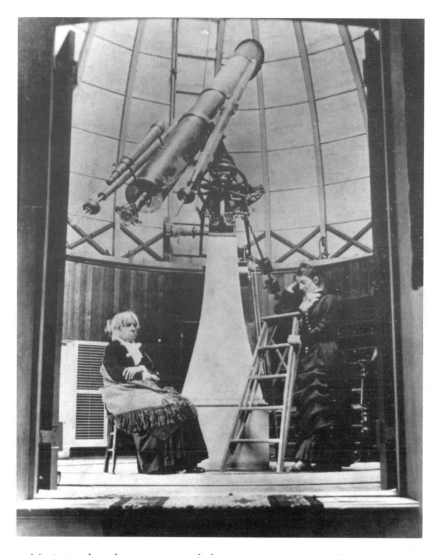

Maria in the observatory with her assistant, Mary Whitney, who
was to follow Maria as Professor of Astronomy at Vassar.
Photo by Vail Brothers, Poughkeepsie, NY, ca. 1877;
courtesy of Special Collections, Vassar College Libraries

After she retired, Maria moved to Lynn, Massachusetts,
and built a small observatory in the backyard of her home.
Photo by W. Marshall Wires; courtesy of
Special Collections, Vassar College Libraries

At the beginning of 1855, Maria's mother fell seriously ill. The family had known Lydia Mitchell only as a strong, hard-working woman, dignified and self-controlled. According to William Mitchell, she had had "a life of uncommon exemption from sickness." It must have been painful for Maria and the rest of them to see this tower of family strength now lying helplessly in bed for weeks on end.

Even before her mother's illness, it had been a sad winter for Maria. She was grieving over the death of three close friends. "I have held the tears just behind my eyelids for a month," she wrote in March, "not being able to cry because of the danger of affecting Mother. . . . I felt when this year came in, a sinking of the heart, as if it had more duties for me, than I could well go through with."

Maria had always been a good nurse, according to Phebe. Now, with Sally and Anne and Phebe married, and Kate soon to go, Maria was the daughter who had to bear most of the burden of caring for their sick mother. Anxious and overworked, Maria found "the little inanities of people who come to the Atheneum to kill time" harder to take than ever. By contrast, her work with the telescope was a relief and a pleasure. "I saw the stars on the evening of the tenth [of February] and met them like old friends from whom I have been long parted — they had been absent from my eyes for three weeks."

By the end of the summer of 1855, Maria was more

determined than ever to give up her once-ideal job at the Atheneum. "I was never more dissatisfied with my life than I have been this summer," she wrote in her diary. "I wish I knew what was best for me to do." Perhaps she longed for the kind of serene confidence that John Greenleaf Whittier described in his poem "First-Day Thoughts":

Cheerful, in the light around me thrown,
Walking as one to pleasant service led;
Doing God's will as if it were my own . . .

In spite of her mother's illness, Maria decided that next year she would take the trip to Europe that she had saved for and planned for so long. In the interim, she worked harder than ever. "I feel constantly hurried because of the shortness of life and I have so much to do — I want thoroughly to understand the subject of perturbations [of the orbits of comets] before I go to Europe and I feel there is an infinitude that I do not know."

By December 16, when they thought that Lydia Mitchell was recovering, Maria noted, "All along this year I have felt that it was a hard year — the hardest of my life." But in a spirit of hope for the new year, she counted her blessings, ending with, "I have saved more money than ever before, hoping for Europe in 1856."

Unfortunately, in 1856 Lydia Mitchell's ill health continued. It was finally decided that Maria should go to

Europe anyway, and the other sisters would take turns nursing their mother. Maria had been offered a chance too good to turn down: a wealthy Chicago banker named H. K. Swift had invited her to chaperone his daughter on travels through the South and Europe. That gave Maria both financial support and a companion (for a respectable woman could not travel by herself).

But then another complication arose. Charles Davis, who had hired Maria as a computer for the *American Ephemeris and Nautical Almanac,* had to tell her that his superior refused to give her leave. If Maria went to Europe, she would lose her job. Davis was vehemently opposed to the decision. "If it depended on me," he wrote indignantly, "you should have a suite of apartments, with a carriage . . . waiting for your arrival in all the principal cities in Europe."

In spite of the threat of losing her job, Maria had her trunk half packed at the beginning of 1857 — but then heavy snow and low temperatures kept Nantucket icebound for almost a month. No mail could get through, including newspapers. "The *Nantucket Inquirer* came out for awhile," Maria noted wryly, "but at length it had nothing to tell and nothing to inquire about, and so kept its peace."

It was overcast most of the time, which prevented telescope work. In fact, the snowdrifts and bitter cold made most kinds of work impossible. Maria and her friends wrote poetry and recited it to each other, played cards and word games such as "Crambo," which requires a player to make up a rhyme to match the opposing player's line. They traded books. Maria sewed herself an entire dress, and her sister Kate made herself a pair of shoes. Finally they were so bored that they began memorizing long poems.

After almost a month of this, the weather turned. The ice softened, and the mail came through. Maria received an important letter: the *American Ephemeris and Nautical Almanac* had decided to allow her to travel and keep her job, on the condition that she take her work with her.

A month later, Maria was on a steamboat pulling out of Nantucket harbor, carrying her away from her friends and relatives and neighbors. The town where she had lived all her life, with the clock tower and the gold cap of the Unitarian church rising above, grew smaller and smaller. After years of planning and dreaming of this moment, Maria Mitchell, now thirty-eight, was launched into the world beyond Nantucket.

CHAPTER 7

The World Beyond Nantucket

Travel had become much faster and easier since Maria Mitchell was born, but it was still slow and uncomfortable. After the all-day steamboat trip from Nantucket to the mainland (a trip that now takes two hours by ferry), she rode a train and then a stagecoach to Meadville, Pennsylvania, for a visit with her now-married sister Phebe. Then Maria took another stagecoach to Erie, the next stop on her way to Chicago to meet the Swifts. In a letter home, she remarked,

> I had, early in life, a love for staging, but it is fast dying out. Nine hours over a rough road are enough to root out the most passionate love of that kind.
>
> Our stage was well filled, but in spite of the solid base we occasionally found ourselves bumping up against the roof or falling forward upon our opposite neighbors.

The bumpiness did not prevent the passengers from discussing politics. Maria soon found out which ones were pro-slavery, which ones anti-slavery. The other major question was who had rooted for newly elected President Buchanan, a Southerner, and who thought Fremont, the Republican Westerner, should have won.

On the overnight train to Chicago, Maria had to sleep on a short wooden bench. Still, she felt guilty because she was so much more comfortable than the many men in the same car who had to ride standing up. In Chicago she picked up Prudence Swift, the young woman she was to chaperone. They took the Illinois Central Railroad to St. Louis and then boarded a steamboat headed down the Mississippi River, into the South.

In the American South, Maria Mitchell found a world more foreign to her, in some ways, than Europe would be. At first the trip was merely full of new sights and experiences. When their steamboat down the Mississippi caught a snag, they had to change boats. Aboard the second steamboat, Maria managed to observe an eclipse of the sun. In Natchez, she was impressed with the romantic scenery and extravagant flowers.

Then, in New Orleans, Maria visited a slave market. She noted with shock one of the slaves to be auctioned, "a girl among them whiter than I, who roused my sympathies very much. I could not speak to her, for the past and the future were too plainly told in her face." When she talked with another slave, "a bright-looking girl of twelve," Maria thought,

58

What right had I to be homesick, when that poor girl had left all her kindred for life without her consent? I could hold my tongue and look around without much outward show of disgust, but to talk pleasantly to the trader I could not consent.

Traveling on through Alabama to Savannah, Georgia, and Charleston, South Carolina, Maria was welcomed with hospitality by the Southerners. However, she was not impressed with their excuses for practicing slavery, and she was appalled at the effect that Southern culture had on the character of the people. She noted the courtesy and agreeable manners of Southern gentlemen, but added, "They also strike me as childlike and fussy. I catch myself feeling that I am the man and they are women; and I see this even in the captain of a steamer. Then they all like to talk sentiment — their religion is a feeling."

Like many tourists in a foreign place, Maria thought she understood Southern culture better than she really did. And perhaps in observing the slaves she trusted her scientific objectivity more than she should have.

When she watched the slaves on a few plantations and in the cities she visited, Maria was not sickened as she had been at the slave market in New Orleans. She concluded that the slaves were not only well treated, but "really happy." "It does not follow," she added, ". . . that slavery is not an evil; and the great evil is, as I always supposed, in the effect upon the whites."

To modern readers, this is a shockingly insensitive

conclusion. Taking it for granted that the slaves hated slavery, we can easily imagine them acting happy in order to survive. We can imagine them concealing their real feelings from a visiting Yankee woman, from their owners — perhaps even from themselves.

Maria had read the novel *Uncle Tom's Cabin* by Harriet Beecher Stowe, with its vivid descriptions of suffering slaves. But she may have distrusted this highly emotional story, as she always distrusted sentimentality. Sadly, on the subject of slavery, Maria Mitchell was more in tune with her times than Harriet Beecher Stowe. In 1857 most white Americans, North and South, believed that there were important differences between blacks and whites — more than just skin color and circumstances.

Of course, most people also believed that women were not equal to men, yet Maria saw through the arguments for keeping women in their place. Some years later, after listening to Professor Peirce of Harvard condescendingly assert that women in science (with the exception perhaps of one) showed no originality, Maria wrote a sharp reply: "If in 1800 years with every advantage some 12 men have been original in science and with every disadvantage one woman has been, the woman's mind must be truly wonderful."

❁   ❁   ❁

At the end of the spring of 1857, Maria Mitchell returned to Nantucket for a few weeks. Mrs. Mitchell had not recovered, but she didn't seem worse, so Maria left for New York. There she met her young charge, Prudence Swift, and they set out again — this time, on the steamship *Arabia,* for Europe. As much as Maria had planned for and dreamed of and longed for this moment, she must have been nervous. "Somebody says, 'Always do what you are afraid to do,'" she wrote in her journal, "and most people are afraid to go to Europe."

But Maria went well prepared. Prestigious friends in America, including Joseph Henry, the director of the Smithsonian Institution, President Everett of Harvard College, and of course Professor Bond of the Harvard Observatory, had written her letters of introduction to the top astronomers of Europe. Maria must have been thrilled to see at last these distant places and people whose influence on her life and work had been so great.

In England, one of her first stops was the Royal Observatory in Greenwich. Here, at zero degrees longitude, the time was set by which the whole world corrected their clocks — the time by which the Mitchells had "rated" the chronometers of the Nantucket whaling fleet. Sir George Airy, the Royal Astronomer at Greenwich, had voted against Maria's winning the gold medal for her discovery of the comet of 1847. But now he welcomed her very cordially, and they became friends.

Another particular highlight was Maria's visit to Collingwood, the home of Sir John Herschel. Herschel was not only an accomplished astronomer himself; he was also the son of the same William Herschel whom all the little Mitchells had believed was the greatest man who ever lived. Proudly Maria wrote her father, "My dear Father, this is Sir John Herschel's place."

The Herschels also welcomed the American astronomer into their household, and they struck up a lasting friendship. Later during her stay in England, someone told Maria that John Herschel's daughter was so well connected by marriage that she was allowed to *sit* in the presence of Queen Victoria. To the democratic Maria, it was rather Queen Victoria who should be honored to associate with the astronomer's daughter.

Another astronomer whom Maria met eagerly was Admiral William Henry Smyth, who had championed Maria's cause in the controversy over the gold medal. He was also the author of *Double Stars,* the subject of which fascinated Maria. She was impressed with Smyth's photographs of the moon, but noted that the English had not yet photographed the stars, as the Bonds at Harvard had.

She also noted that Smyth was a hard worker, but he was unusual for an amateur astronomer in England — most of them were wealthy men who kept their telescopes mainly for show. In America, thought Maria, amateur astronomers were usually people like her father, without spare money or leisure time. "A poor schoolmaster, who has some bright boys who ask questions, buys a glass and becomes a star-gazer . . . or a watchmaker must know the time, and therefore watches the stars as time-keepers. In almost all cases they are hard-working men."

When she visited Cambridge University, Maria was pleased to meet John Couch Adams, who had mathematically deduced the existence and the location of the planet Neptune. But since the Royal Astronomer had not announced Adams's results promptly, a Frenchman, Urbain Jean Joseph Leverrier, had published his similar calculations first. (Furthermore, J. G. Galle, assistant director of the Berlin Observatory, was the first to actually sight the eighth planet.) Leverrier had been given the honors for the discovery, and there was still bad feeling between the English and the French over this.

English literature as well as science had deeply influenced Maria, and so she traveled to Stratford-on-Avon to pay homage to Shakespeare. She also made a pilgrimage to Sir Walter Scott's former home, where she was overcome with homesickness, perhaps because Scott's novels had been so much a part of her childhood. "The clouds came up and the wind howled when we came out [of the house]," she wrote, "and as we climbed the ascent to the woods where we had left the carriage, I had half a mind to sit down and cry."

In London, Maria visited Westminster Abbey, where she stopped reverently at the grave of Joseph Addison, the poet who had written "The spacious firmament on high." While in London she also found the house where Dr. Samuel Johnson, the author of the famous *Dictionary*, had died. And she sought out the house of the great seventeenth-century scientist Isaac Newton. "Newton seems to combine all the best qualities of the men of science near his time," she wrote in her diary later. "He was a more discriminating observer than Tycho Brahe [a sixteenth-century astronomer, the most accurate observer of his time] or Kepler [the seventeenth century astronomer who discovered the laws of planetary motion] — a sounder philosopher than Galileo, a mathematician whose like the world has not seen and a follower of truth wherever it led him. And withal so simple and modest." Interestingly, most of the qualities that Maria admired in Newton were the same qualities that others admired in her.

Before Maria Mitchell and Prudence Swift could start for France, word came from across the Atlantic of a financial crash in America caused by an influx of California gold and overspeculation in land and railroads. H. K. Swift, Prudence's father, had gone bankrupt, and Prudence had to return home. But Maria was determined to explore the rest of Europe, even though now her budget would be tight. She saw Prudence off on the steamer to New York and began looking for an escort so she could travel on to Paris.

The highlight of Maria's stay in Paris should have been her visit to the astronomer Leverrier at the Paris Observatory. But at that time the French scientists and the English scientists were still quarreling over who really deserved the credit for discovering Neptune, and perhaps Leverrier associated Maria with the English. Or perhaps he was unwilling to take a woman scientist seriously. In any case, he received Maria socially and showed her around the observatory as if she were a tourist, but he did not let her into the domes.

After only a few weeks in France, Maria was eager to go on to Rome, but she needed someone to travel with. Luckily she had already met the author Nathaniel Hawthorne in England, and now she heard that the Hawthornes were in Paris, about to depart for Rome.

Hawthorne might have been a famous author, but he was an odd — and odd-looking — man. "His hair stands out on each side," wrote Maria, "so much so that one's thoughts naturally turn to combs and hair-brushes." She had tried to discuss religion, a constant interest of hers, with Hawthorne, but "I never could get at anything of his religious views."

Hawthorne was not especially sociable, but he had taken a liking to Maria. He assured his wife, who was not in good health, that Miss Mitchell "would give no trouble" as a traveling companion.

By the time they reached Rome, Maria had become good friends with all the Hawthornes, including their eleven-year-old son Julian, who adored her. She saw them almost every day, becoming an honorary member of the family. Hawthorne, who at that time was at work on his novel *The Marble Faun,* put her into the book in a reference to a woman astronomer. "The woman's eye," he wrote, "that has discovered a new star, turns from its glory to send the polished little instrument [a needle] gleaming along the hem of her kerchief or to darn a casual fray in her dress." Maria was amused at this description, since she did *not* share Hawthorne's sentimentality about women sewing. She remarked to a friend later that the dress Hawthorne had seen her working on was probably badly mended.

In Rome, Maria visited the spot where, in the seventeenth century, the assembled cardinals of the Church of Rome had forced Galileo to take back his statement that the earth revolved around the sun. She wrote,

> I knew of no sadder picture in the history of science than that of the old man, Galileo, worn by a long life of scientific research, weak and feeble, trembling before that tribunal whose frown was torture, and declaring that to be false which he knew to be true. And I know of no picture in the history of religion more weakly pitiable than that of the Holy Church trembling before Galileo, and denouncing him because he found in the Book of Nature truths not stated in their own Book of God — forgetting that the Book of Nature is also a Book of God.
>
> It seems to be difficult for any one to take in the idea that two truths cannot conflict.

In spite of the way Maria felt about the Church's treatment of Galileo, she was eager to visit the Vatican Observatory. But she had to wait for weeks, because the observatory was also a monastery, as Father Angelo

Secchi, the astronomer, explained. No woman was allowed there unless she had special permission from a
cardinal. Both Sir John Herschel's daughter and the
mathematician and astronomer Mary Somerville had
been denied entrance.

Finally, a young Italian acquaintance of Maria's, the
nephew of a monseigneur, persuaded his uncle to cut
through the red tape and get the letter Maria needed
from a cardinal. Once official permission had been
granted, Father Secchi was glad to show Maria the
observatory. She was impressed at how well she was
able to see Jupiter and Saturn, even in broad daylight,
with the powerful Vatican telescope.

"I should have been glad to stay until dark to look
at nebulae," wrote Maria, "but the Father kindly informed me that my permission did not extend beyond
the daylight, which was fast leaving us, and conducting
me to the door he informed me that I must make my
way home alone, adding, 'But we live in a civilized
country.' "

Independent American though she was, Maria knew
it was discourteous to expect a woman to make her way
through the streets of a foreign city, in the evening,
without any escort. "I did not express to him the doubt
that rose to my thoughts!"

CHAPTER 8

A Magnificent Enterprise

Maria Mitchell felt more at home in Rome than in any other part of Europe. But she had been traveling for over a year, and she missed Nantucket. In a letter to a friend, she wrote, "Even in Rome, and after 8 months in Europe, I think our Nantucket people are bright. . . . If I think well of the Nantucketers intellectually after 'seeing the model' I must think well of them morally. I really believe that there are few communities in the world to compare with it in this respect."

Before she left Europe, Maria visited Mary Somerville, the British mathematician and astronomer whose work *Physical Geography* had gained her international recognition. This renowned woman was now seventy-seven, but she and Maria found much to discuss, including the connection of astronomy to life after death. "I have no doubt," said Somerville about heavenly bodies, "that in another state of existence we shall know more about these things."

Maria then traveled to Berlin to visit Alexander von Humboldt, the famous scientist whose work *Cosmos* she had pored over, years earlier, in the Atheneum. He, like Maria, admired Mary Somerville. He was eager to hear about how far American astronomers had progressed in photographing the stars. To Maria's embarrassment, he was more up-to-date than she was on current events in the United States. He seemed well informed about the current burning issue — whether Kansas would be admitted to the Union as a slave state.

❂   ❂   ❂

Maria finally returned home to Nantucket in the summer of 1858. She found her mother's health still no worse — but no better — than it had been a year ago. Maria again took her place at her mother's bedside, a place she would keep for the next three years.

On the brighter side, in 1859 Maria was presented with a wonderful gift: a high-quality five-inch telescope, bought for her by a women's group. She was deeply touched by this recognition, and afterward she spoke of "the noble woman [Elizabeth Peabody] . . . acting for the 'Women of America'" as one of three people outside her family who had "made epochs in my life."

As the years of her mother's illness wore on, Maria found relief in her study of the heavens. She continued her work for the *American Ephemeris and Nautical Almanac,* which she had kept up faithfully all the time she was in Europe. European as well as American friends had suggestions about how Maria ought to use her fine new telescope. W. H. Smyth, the author of *Double Stars,* wrote urging her to make a study of the colors of binary star systems (systems consisting of two stars). J. I. Bowditch, son of Nathaniel Bowditch, whose *New American Practical Navigator* Maria had pored over in the Atheneum, wrote from Boston. He hoped Maria would "look out sharp for the interior planet." (He was referring to "Vulcan," the theoretical planet presumed to be inside the orbit of Mercury.)

In April of 1860 Maria wrote to Phebe about the work she was doing:

> I've been intensely busy. I have been looking for the little inferior planet to cross the sun, which it hasn't done, and I got an article ready for the paper and then hadn't the courage to publish — not for fear of the readers, but for fear that I should change my own ideas by the time 'twas in print.
>
> I am hoping, however, to have something by the meeting of the Scientific Association in August, — some paper, — not to get reputation for myself, — my reputation is so much beyond me that as policy I should keep quiet, — but in order that my telescope may show that it is at work.

❁   ❁   ❁

In 1861, a few months before the Confederate guns firing on Fort Sumter set off the Civil War, Lydia Mitchell died. Her mind had been wandering for some time, although William Mitchell believed that just before her death she was lucid and peaceful. But for Maria and her father, it must have been a harrowing period. And they were evidently desperate to get away.

For both Maria (in her early forties now) and her father, Nantucket was the home where they had grown and flourished, and they had also helped the community of Nantucket grow and flourish. But these days, without the whaling industry or in fact much of any industry, Nantucket was looking more and more like a ghost town. It was no longer the same Nantucket that Maria had missed while she was in Europe, but a melancholy place of memories. And their most recent memories were of Lydia's long illness and death.

In the short space of three months, Maria and her father concluded all their business on Nantucket and left the island. They would come back to visit, but Nantucket would never be their home again. Hoping for a fresh start, they moved to the Boston area, to a little house in Lynn. Maria's sister Kate and her family were already settled there. Besides, as Mr. Mitchell noted, "Maria had been for years desirous of living in Boston."

The trouble with this fresh start was that Maria and her father were followed by their grief. The next four years must have been a strange, dreary period for them.

Besides enduring their private sorrow, they were living in a country that was threatening to tear itself apart in the Civil War. The war even divided the Mitchell family. Maria's older brother Andrew served in the Union Navy. But one of her younger brothers, William Forster, who was still a Quaker, could not condone the war even for the purpose of ending slavery. He was sickened by a battle he observed, and he was never "able to see how it is possible for a soldier to be a Christian."

During this period Maria "was very much depressed by her mother's death," Phebe wrote, "and absorbed herself as much as possible in her observations and in her work for the *Nautical Almanac.*" Mr. Mitchell, now in his seventies, served on the Board of Overseers of the Harvard Observatory and also as chairman of the Harvard Observatory Committee. But he was also depressed, suffering during those four years, in his own words, "many periods of irrepressible gloom." Maria and her father set up their own backyard observatory and continued their work, but some of the zest had gone out of even their lifelong passion for astronomy.

Perhaps during these years Maria wondered if the best part of her life was already over. Perhaps she wondered if she would end up like Dorothea Dix, the reformer, respected and successful in her work, but alone.

❁   ❁   ❁

The one hopeful sign on Maria Mitchell's horizon was a bold and ambitious project for women's education. Matthew Vassar, a wealthy brewer in Poughkeepsie, New York, was founding a college for women. "I wish to give to one sex," he explained to his trustees, "the advantages too long monopolized by the other." Unlike many of his time, Vassar believed that "woman, having received from her creator the same intellectual constitution as man, has the same right as man to intellectual culture and development."

Construction of the buildings of Vassar Female College, as it was called at first, began during the Civil War. At that time labor and materials were scarce and expensive. Still, Vassar was determined to give his school all the facilities of a first-rate college. The grounds were landscaped to look like the Tuileries Gardens in Paris; the main building, where the students and most of the faculty would live, was designed to resemble the Hotel de Ville, also in Paris.

The observatory was a state-of-the-art structure, meant to rival those of Harvard and Yale. The walls of the main section were solid brick, for stability, and shock-proof piers and stone pedestals supported the telescopes and other instruments. The main telescope boasted a lens of twelve and three-eighths inches in aperture. The mighty dome of the observatory, covered with sheet tin, weighed one-and-a-half tons, but could be revolved "very easily by an arrangement of sixteen cast-iron pulleys," as Benson Lossing, a trustee of the college, described it.

To get his college off to the right start, Matthew Vassar wanted to assemble a faculty as outstanding as his buildings. For Professor of Astronomy and Director of the Observatory, he wanted Maria Mitchell.

"I can but be gratified that you should think me fitted to fill so responsible a position," Maria wrote to the Reverend Rufus Babcock, Vassar's agent. "The whole enterprise is magnificent." A month later she wrote to Matthew Vassar himself, saying, "In common with every intelligent person in the country I have watched with great interest the progress of your enterprise, and have rejoiced in the belief that a solid education would be afforded to American women — such as they have never yet known."

Maria was strongly attracted to the idea of being part of this "magnificent enterprise," and lured by the prospect of running such a fine new observatory. But she hesitated to accept the position. She worried about moving her father again — would he be happy at Vassar? She was also concerned that teaching would take time away from her own astronomy work. On the other hand, as she told Babcock, "I should hope, in time, to find students who would tax my utmost powers, and it will be strange if Vassar College does not bring out some girls who shall go far beyond me."

Modest as usual, Maria also worried about whether she was qualified to teach at the college level. No one else had any such doubts. Some top people in higher education in New England, including Professor Peirce of Harvard, offered glowing recommendations for her.

"If your Institution intends to teach Science truly and thoroughly," wrote President Alexis Caswell of Brown University, "it will be fortunate in securing the service of Miss Mitchell." Alphonsus Crosby of the Salem Normal School was even more complimentary: "Her distinguished scientific attainments, her liberal literary culture, the remarkable success and honors which she has already attained, her signal industry and zeal in the promotion of science, her frankness and ease of personal communication, her acquaintance with the institutions and savants of our own and other lands, and her beautiful simplicity and benevolence of character, unite in recommending her as eminently fitted."

Maria wrote one particular letter to Babcock, Vassar's agent, for which she must have been sorry later. "I had not thought of so large a sum [$1500 per year] as you say the President supposes I shall require. I do not believe I am worth it!" At the same time, Maria worried about how she would earn her living if she were unsuccessful at college teaching. She finally decided to accept the job at Vassar but continue her work for the *Nautical Almanac,* just in case.

And so, in the summer of 1865, Maria and her father traveled by steamboat up the Hudson River from New York City to Poughkeepsie. The dramatic scenery of the bluffs and steep hills along the river must have seemed fitting for this dramatic moment in their lives. On the brand-new campus of Vassar Female College, they settled into their quarters in the red-brick observatory with its gleaming tin dome.

In September, when Vassar opened its doors, Maria Mitchell (now forty-seven) faced her first class in astronomy. To these young women she must have been a striking figure, even in her simple white shirtwaist and black skirt, with a piece of lace pinned on her gray curls. One student described her as "dignified, imposing, at times almost overpowering." Perhaps it was the direct gaze of her large, dark eyes, "strangely deepset." Or maybe it was not so much how she looked as what she said to these young women.

In case they had any misunderstandings about astronomy, she set them straight. "Star-gazing is not science. The entrance to astronomy is through mathematics. You must make up your mind to steady and earnest work. You must be content to get on slowly if you only get on thoroughly." Professor Mitchell knew what she was talking about. This was the way she had "got on" herself, slowly and thoroughly, in long hours of study in the Nantucket Atheneum. She made her students feel that they could do it, too.

But Maria also made decidedly unmathematical assertions. She startled her students by saying, "We especially need imagination in science. It is not all mathematics, nor all logic, but it is somewhat beauty and poetry." Even more startling was this declaration: "Every formula which expresses a law of nature is a hymn of praise to God."

No wonder that one student said, "A chance meeting with Miss Mitchell . . . always gave me an electric shock."

CHAPTER 9

Women Studying Together

Not everyone agreed with Matthew Vassar that woman had "the same intellectual constitution as man." In 1864, a writer in a Boston magazine, criticizing the proposed curriculum at Vassar, expressed what many people believed: "We should as soon think of putting a hod of bricks on the shoulders of a young daughter of our own and compel her to climb a ladder with it three times a day as for the same period to impose on her brain the mental burden of these studies."

Two of the studies supposed to place an especially weighty burden on the female brain were higher mathematics and astronomy. Professor Maria Mitchell made it plain she thought this was nonsense. Nor was she about to offer a watered-down version of her subject, the "popular science" thought more suitable for ladies. "That knowledge which is popular is not scientific," she told her students. "The laws which govern the motions of the sun, the earth, planets, and other bodies in the universe, cannot be understood and demonstrated without a solid basis of mathematical learning."

Maria showed her students a respect for their minds that many of them had never before experienced. She assumed, for instance, that they were capable of studying the textbooks for themselves, instead of having the contents spoon-fed to them in lectures. She later wrote,

My students used to say that my way of teaching was like that of the man who said to his son, "There are the letters of the English alphabet — go into that corner and learn them."

It is not exactly my way, but I do think, as a general rule, that teachers talk too much! A book is a very good institution! To read a book, to think it over, and to write out notes is a useful exercise; a book which will not repay some hard thought is not worth publishing. The fashion of lecturing is becoming a rage; the teacher shows herself off, and she does not try enough to develop her pupils.

In spite of her harsh words about lectures, Maria's own lectures were lively and inspiring. Often she presented ideas, such as the following, that must have seemed revolutionary to her students.

There is this great danger in student life. Now, we rest all upon what Socrates said, or what Copernicus taught; how can we dispute authority which has come down to us, all established, for ages?

We must at least question it; we cannot accept anything as granted, beyond the first mathematical formulae. Question everything else.

Maria herself was the best evidence that women could not only learn but excel in mathematics and astronomy. And by her way of teaching, she invited her students to discover their own abilities. To the senior class in astronomy of 1876 she expressed what had been her attitude from the day the college opened its doors: "We are women studying together."

※　　※　　※

By 1868 Maria Mitchell must have realized how much the young women who came to Vassar needed a teacher like her. On October 15 of that year she wrote in her diary, "Resolved, in case of my outliving father and being in good health, to give my efforts to the intellectual culture of women, without regard to salary." She did not make this resolution lightly, because it meant giving up a certain amount of her work as an independent scientist. "The scientist should be free to pursue his investigations," she explained later. "He cannot be a scientist and a school-master." Her resolution also meant giving up her work for the *Nautical Almanac* and depending on her salary at Vassar to support herself and her father.

Maria's students responded to her high expectations with enthusiastic hard work. One student felt that Maria's very parlor in the observatory, with its bust of the mathematician Mary Somerville and its shelves of books by famous scientists and novelists and poets whom Maria knew personally, "conveyed a new conception of severe scholarship, that gave [a new student] a fresh and inspiring glimpse of the possible attainments of women; and yet . . . with its flowers and sunshine and warm colors was thoroughly human and friendly."

Many of the students came to Vassar from homes where "severe scholarship" was the last thing expected of them. At a reception for new students and their mothers, one anxious mother burst into tears. She confided in Maria about her daughter: "She is not a Christian. I know I put her into good hands when I put her here."

"Then I was strongly tempted to avow my Unitarianism," wrote Maria. The mother went on, "And, Miss Mitchell, will you ask Miss Lyman to insist that my daughter shall curl her hair? She looks very graceful when her hair is curled, and I want it insisted upon." Maria tried to keep a straight face as she made a note of the mother's request, but when she caught the eye of another teacher, she burst out laughing.

In fact, the students *were* in good hands with Maria Mitchell. "Homesick 'new girls' on the well known first north transverse [of Main Building] rejoiced in her," wrote Frances Wood, a teacher at Vassar, "and blessed her for want of ceremony in rapping on their doors nearly every day the first week or two with the cheery inquiry, 'How are you getting on?' and 'Can I help you in any way?'" One student later wrote, "What one remembers longest of Miss Mitchell . . . is that beautiful smile that broke with a soft light over her rugged face, with a look of perfect kindness. . . . [There was] a tenderness in her that was not only womanly — it was motherly."

But there was another woman at Vassar College, Principal Hannah Lyman, whose job it was to supervise the social, physical, and spiritual life of the students. Miss Lyman's ideas were quite different from Professor Mitchell's. For instance, Miss Lyman wanted the young ladies in bed with the lights out at ten o'clock, but if there was an astronomical event to be observed, Maria would rouse her students out of bed without asking anyone's permission. During the meteor shower of November 1868, Maria and five student observers stayed up all night. "The minute from 2:24 to 2:25 [a.m.] was the most fruitful," Maria noted coolly in her report.

Miss Lyman inspected all the students' dresses to make sure they were long enough to cover their shoes. "Young ladies are not supposed to have feet," she declared. By this Miss Lyman meant that it was not modest or ladylike for a young woman to show her feet.

In contrast, Maria not only had feet but did not worry about showing them. In photographs of her sitting on the steps to the observatory dome with her students, her sturdy boots are plain to see. For comfort, she liked to wear oversize shoes.

Miss Lyman's first concern for the young women in her care was that they be Christian in her sense of the word — any girl who broke a rule was not only reproved but prayed over. Her second concern was that young women should comport themselves like ladies. Her distant third concern was that they apply themselves to their studies. Naturally, Miss Lyman was often upset with Professor Mitchell, although of course in a "Christian" and ladylike way.

Maria's assessment of Miss Lyman was typically frank: "Miss [Lyman] is a bigot, but a very sincere one. She is the most conservative person I ever met. I think her a very good woman, a woman of great energy. . . . She is very kind to me, but had we lived in the colonial days of Massachusetts, and had she been a power, she would have burned me at the stake for heresy!"

Cornelia Raymond, the youngest daughter of John Raymond, the president of Vassar, was soon intimate friends with Miss Mitchell. The little girl did not share Miss Lyman's probable assessment of Maria Mitchell's spiritual standing. Cornelia had the firm expectation, even later in life, that "one of the first things I shall hear in Heaven will be her deep voice saying, 'Well, little Nellie, here we are.'"

There were a few students at Vassar who criticized Professor Mitchell — as much for unladylike behavior as for heresy. One of these (not an astronomy student) was heard to remark that Professor Mitchell "was no doubt a great woman, but as a lady she did not think very much of her." But criticism like this was more than offset by the ardent response of most students to Maria Mitchell. "For my part," retorted Mary King Babbitt indignantly, "I would no more have pinned down Professor Mitchell's manners to meet the requirements of a book of etiquette, than I would have changed her face. . . . Notwithstanding her informal manner with the students, I think no one of them ever ventured to speak to her or of her, or to think of her with anything but the utmost respect."

One way in which Maria respected her students was to give them serious work in applied astronomy. Her senior students obtained the correct time for the college by measuring the apparent motion of certain stars. Counting meteors in a meteor shower was not just an exercise; the results that Maria and her students obtained were reported to the scientific community and increased the store of scientific knowledge.

With her own money Mitchell bought equipment for photographing the sun, to monitor sun spots, and trained her students to operate it. She required them to "find a planet at any hour of the day, to make drawings of what they see, and to determine positions of planets and satellites. . . . They make, sometimes, very accurate drawings, and they learn to know the satellites of Saturn (Titan, Rhea, etc.) by their different physiognomy, as they would persons. They have sometimes measured diameters."

In 1869, Maria led a group of her students to Iowa to observe an eclipse of the sun. Proud of their professional work during the eclipse, she noted at the end of her report, "Piazzi Smyth [Charles Piazzi Smyth, Astronomer Royal of Scotland and son of W. H. Smyth] says, 'The effect of a total eclipse on the minds of men is so overpowering, that if they have never seen it before they forget their appointed tasks, and *will* look around during the few seconds of total obscuration, to witness the scene.' Other astronomers have said the same. My assistants, a party of young students, would not have turned from the narrow line of observation assigned to them if the earth had quaked beneath them. . . . Was it because they were *women?*"

In her new home at Vassar, Maria's social life blossomed. She made friends not only with her students but also with other professors, teachers, and others connected with the college. Even some who disagreed with her views on such topics as religion, science, and women's education, including Trustee Elias Magoon and President John Raymond, became good friends. Matthew Vassar himself was a frequent visitor to the observatory.

❁   ❁   ❁

Before long it seemed that none of Maria Mitchell's worries about accepting the job at Vassar had been justified. She was a resounding success as a teacher, and her salary was assured. And her father was happy for the first time in years.

If Maria was a mother to her students, Mr. Mitchell was their grandfather. Surrounded by bright young women and able to enjoy the company of the founder Matthew Vassar and President Raymond and all the many interesting people who lived at and visited the college, William Mitchell was supremely content. Maria, tongue in cheek, informed the principal, Miss Lyman, that "my father is so much pleased with everything here that I am afraid he will be immersed [baptized]!" Maria did not record whether Miss Lyman, who was a Baptist, laughed at the joke.

But this happy period for Maria and her father lasted only a few years. Toward the end of 1868, William Mitchell became ill. He died the following April, full of gratitude for a good life and serenely expecting to meet his wife and other loved ones who had gone on ahead of him.

For her part, Maria was stunned with grief. William was not only her father; he was her oldest friend and colleague. She could not imagine life without him. After the funeral, which was held on Nantucket, she wrote John Raymond, the president of Vassar, "I feel the need of more than one day of quiet, before I enter upon the new and incomprehensible life before me."

Maria was now fifty. More urgently than before, she wanted to know if there was life after death. Frances

Wood, a good friend of Maria's at Vassar, remembered the Sunday evening discussions of the small group of faculty who had Unitarian leanings. "'No matter what we resolve to talk about,' [Maria] said laughingly, 'we always seem to end up with the immortality of the soul.' This subject had a fascination for her and she was fond of getting 'views' as she called it from persons she valued."

But other people's "views" never quite managed to convince Maria once and for all, much as she may have wished for a serene faith like her father's. Her mind refused to accept as fact what could not be proven. "Let us have truth," she wrote later, "even if the truth be the awful denial of the good God. We must face the light and not bury our heads in the earth. I am hopeful that scientific investigation, pushed on and on, will reveal new ways in which God works, and bring to us deeper revelations of the wholly unknown."

CHAPTER 10

More than Astronomy

Years before, when she was still working at the Nantucket Atheneum, Maria Mitchell had written, "To know what one ought to do is certainly the hardest thing in life. 'Doing' is comparatively easy." At Vassar College, introducing young women to the discipline and "poetry" of astronomy, she seemed to feel she had finally discovered what she ought to do. It was a joy and at the same time a solemn duty. Her sense of a mission in teaching must have helped pull her through her grief over her father's death.

In September of 1871, Maria wrote, "My classes came in to-day for the first time; twenty-five students — more than ever before; fine, splendid-looking girls. I felt almost frightened at the responsibility which came into my hands — of the possible *twist* which I might give them."

There was one "twist" that Maria did not hesitate to give her girls: exposure to the women's movement. Maria was friends with many of the foremost workers for women's rights, and she invited them to Vassar. Julia Ward Howe recited "The Battle Hymn of the Republic" to the Vassar student body, and Mary Livermore described her work in military hospitals during the Civil War. Maria's students were also privileged to meet Louisa May Alcott, Lucy Stone, and Elizabeth Cady Stanton, among others, in smaller gatherings at the observatory. Maria's friend Frances Wood remembered fondly those evenings of "spirited talk and free discussion" with distinguished guests. "What personal anecdote and reminiscence! And what good coffee at the end!"

The shy young Maria who had avoided social gatherings had grown into a mature and more socially comfortable woman who became a giver of parties. The most famous of these were her yearly "Dome Parties," which she held each June in the dome of the observatory for her astronomy students. Little tables set with place cards and roses from Maria's garden were arranged under the great equatorial telescope, and the students were treated to such delights as strawberries, ice cream, and cake. Maria, who was clever at making up verses, presented each girl with a poem composed especially for her. Then Maria would hand out pencils and paper and have them all make up verses.

In the 1870s two of her students took the spirit of these games a step further. They brought to one Dome Party an entire song about Maria Mitchell, set to the tune of "The Battle Hymn of the Republic." "We are singing for the glory of Maria Mitchell's name," it began. The second verse went like this:

> She leads us thro' the mazes of hard Astronomy,
> She teaches us Nutation and the laws
> > of Kepler three,
> Th'inclination of their orbits and their eccentricity,
> Good woman that she be.
> > *Chorus:* Glory, glory, hallelujah . . .

Maria was delighted — this was just the kind of fooling around with words and rhymes that she appreciated. "It is true," she said. "I am not a wise woman, but I am a good one." The song became a tradition at Dome Parties.

Maria had already launched some students who would have an impact on science and women's education in this country. Christine Ladd-Franklin, Vassar class of 1869, was the first woman allowed to study for a Ph.D. in mathematics at Johns Hopkins University; she made a significant contribution to the field of symbolic logic. Ellen Swallow Richards, class of 1870, was given special permission to study chemistry at the Massachusetts Institute of Technology, and became the first woman to receive a B.S. degree. She would become a leader in the application of chemistry to living conditions and in the development of home economics.

In spite of the deep satisfaction Maria Mitchell gained from her work and from association with her students, life at Vassar had its trials. For one thing, the much-heralded observatory, supposed to be one of the best in the country, had continual maintenance problems. The mechanism that was supposed to allow the ponderous dome to revolve "very easily" actually needed a strong man to operate it. Another problem was the "driving apparatus of the telescope," as Maria wrote trustee Benson Lossing. "Accuracy cannot be obtained in measurement."

The college always seemed reluctant to part with the money for repairs or new equipment. Sometimes Maria gave up and used her own money, or asked friends or acquaintances for donations.

Another problem was housing. Maria and her father (when he was alive) had lived in the observatory ever since they first came to Vassar College. As far as astronomy went, the observatory was the most convenient place for Maria to live, since she often stayed up late or rose before dawn to watch the skies. However, the observatory had been designed as a place of scientific study rather than as a home, and it was never really comfortable. Furthermore, Maria had to keep going to the college with requests for more coal for heat or for more adequate furnishings. In 1875 Maria complained to the college in a report, "My own accommodations are exceedingly limited and poor." Part of her living quarters in the observatory were being used for a classroom, and part for student housing. At one point she was sleeping on the sofa in the parlor (which was also a classroom). A student composed a sarcastic poem to commemorate the end of this housing situation. The refrain of the poem went, "Miss Mitchell sleeps in a bed!"

Another kind of trial for Maria was the differences between her and her colleagues. The other faculty sometimes found Professor Mitchell odd and difficult, and she sometimes lost patience with them. During her second year at Vassar, she noted in her diary, "Our faculty meetings always try me in this respect: we do things that other colleges have done before. We wait and ask for precedent. If the earth had waited for a precedent, it never would have turned on its axis." She didn't believe in giving grades ("You cannot mark a human mind") or honors ("The whole system is demoralizing and foolish. Girls study for prizes and not for learning, when 'honors' are at the end."). Furthermore, Maria deliberately arrived at faculty meetings a few minutes late to avoid the opening prayers, which she considered an empty form.

Maria also resented any criticism, spoken or unspoken, of the way she dressed. Once a teacher, meaning to be helpful, picked a stray white thread off Maria's gray shawl — and was sternly rebuked. "Please put that back just where you took it from! I consider it an impertinence!"

John Raymond, who was president of Vassar from 1864 to 1878, thought of Maria Mitchell as a "bright, unwavering star" of Vassar College, and the two became good friends. But Raymond was extremely concerned that Vassar students might lose what he considered their femininity in the process of developing their minds. In a baccalaureate sermon he delivered, he told the graduating women that "in certain respects, woman is, must be, ought to be, subordinate to man." He justified this idea by quoting Jesus: "Whoever will be chief among you, let him be your servant." (Why this did not apply equally to men was not clear.)

The subordination of women to men applied to the professors' salaries, as Maria Mitchell and Alida Avery, the college physician and professor of physiology, soon found out. In the nineteenth century, there was plenty of "precedent" for this kind of unfairness. Most women — if they were even allowed to do the same work as men — expected unequal salaries, and would never have dreamed of protesting. But to Maria Mitchell, such reasons as "it isn't the way" were no reason at all.

In May of 1870, Maria and Alida Avery, the only two women professors, wrote Raymond a formal letter of protest:

> We desire to call your attention to the fact that, after nearly five years of what we believe to be faithful working for the good of the College, our pay is still far below that which has been offered *at entrance,* to the other professors, even when they have been wholly inexperienced.

> We respectfully ask that our salaries may be made equal to those of the other professors.

In June, the board of trustees refused their request, offering some dubious reasoning and dubious arithmetic. But Maria and her colleague didn't give up, and the argument continued on into 1871. The two women seriously considered leaving the college, until finally their salaries were raised (although they still weren't equal to the men's).

Religion was another sore point. Matthew Vassar had founded Vassar as a nonsectarian college, and the board of trustees was well aware of his intent. But in fact, Maria's sister Phebe noted, the college was "mainly under Baptist control."

As for Maria, she resolved early on to "connect myself with liberal Christian institutions, believing as I do that happiness and growth in this life are best promoted by them and that what is good in this life is good in any life." She and a few like-minded faculty members formed a discussion group that they nicknamed "the Rads," short for "Radicals."

Many were offended by Maria's lack of conventional piety. A missionary who asked, "Miss Mitchell, what is your favorite position in prayer?" got the answer "Flat on my back!" Noting that a student had, in all seriousness, pinned the scriptural motto "Seek and ye shall find" on her wardrobe, Maria commented dryly, "Most likely not find."

Worse, Maria didn't seem to think the required twice-daily chapel attendance was very worthwhile. When a fellow teacher complained to her, she sym-

pathized and offered this advice: "Oh, well, do as *I* do
— sit back folding your arms, and think of something
pleasant!"

But when chapel attendance conflicted with the
work of the astronomy department, Mitchell was not
so resigned. She wrote President Raymond saucy notes
such as the following:

> My good natured President,
>   I want to hear you preach tomorrow, and I also want
> to see the moon pass over Aldebaran. [Here she in-
> cluded a little sketch of the moon approaching the star.]
> Can't you let me do both? Will you stop at eleventhly
> or twelfthly? Or, why need you show us *all* sides of the
> subject? The moon never turns to us other than the
> one side we see, and did you ever know a finer moon?

President Raymond was indeed good-natured, and he
liked and respected Maria despite their differences of
opinion. But there were some who were outraged that
Maria Mitchell was even allowed to teach at the college.
After Raymond's death in 1878, trustee Nathan Bishop
wrote a secret letter to the new president, implying that
Professor Mitchell ought to be fired. "I was aware that
Miss Mitchell was a 'rank Theodore Parker Unitarian'
when she was elected. I believe she has kept away from
Vassar five times as many students as her influence has
drawn to it."

Maria would not have been insulted to be associated

with the abolitionist and social reformer Theodore Parker. And although she was not actually a member of any denomination, her sympathies were with the Unitarians. But she took religion more seriously than many more conventional Christians.

In spite of her flip remark about leaning back during chapel and thinking about something pleasant, Maria actually thought a great deal about what the preachers said. Some of them might have been uneasy if they had realized what attentive criticism their words were receiving from the woman with the silver curls and the sedate Quaker-like dress. About one preacher who "cried, or pretended to cry, at the pathetic points" in his sermon, Maria commented, "I hope he really cried, for a weakness is better than an affectation of weakness."

Preaching about original sin was sure to make Maria angry. "If God made me, and made me evil, he must take the consequences," she wrote tartly. But she went on in a serious vein: "I don't think he made me evil — but what is evil and how did it come into existence — is it only the opposite of Good?"

"She had a deeply religious nature," said Frances Wood, Maria's friend and fellow "Rad." "And how quickly she responded to what was noble and uplifting in any service!" Wood remembered attending a service in New York City with Maria one Easter vacation, and the preacher's invocation: "Let us come into thy presence this morning, forgetting all bitter memories of the past; the cares, anxieties and trials of the present; the gloomy forebodings of the future; and ascend with Thee into that higher realm where the sun is always shining, and where love never wanes." This must have been exactly what Maria needed to hear that morning. She whispered to Wood, "I am full fed now, — could go home this minute."

When the Scottish author and preacher George Mac-Donald visited Vassar in 1873, Mitchell was deeply moved by his talks at chapel. "He took those of us who were *emotional* completely — not by storm so much as by gentle breezes," she wrote. "In his sermon he said, 'Don't trouble yourself about what you *believe*, but *do* the will of God.' His consciousness of the existence of God and of his immediate supervision was felt every minute by those who listened."

To many at Vassar, however, belief in specific doctrines was all-important. One source of conflict between Maria Mitchell and the conservative faculty and trustees was Charles Darwin's new theory of evolution. The conservatives thought the theory was blasphemous because it contradicted their literal interpretation of Scripture. Maria saw it simply as a theory, to be judged on the evidence like any scientific theory. She was baffled that others actually seemed afraid of Darwin, much as the Church had once feared Galileo.

After listening to a preacher denounce "the doctrines of scientists" as "some of the dangers that threaten us," Maria wrote in her diary, "I was most surprised at his fear. . . . Can the study of truth do harm? Does not every true scientist seek only to know the truth? And in our deep ignorance of what is truth, shall we dread the search for it?"

❂   ❂   ❂

In 1873, Maria Mitchell took a second trip to Europe. This time she visited Russia, accompanied by her nephew William Kendall, Phebe's son. Her main purpose was to visit the renowned observatory at Pulkovo, near St. Petersburg. There she was welcomed cordially by the director, Otto von Struve.

Maria was also interested in Russian culture. As she wrote, "I try, when I am abroad, to see in what they are superior to us, — not in what they are inferior." She was impressed with the Russian government's respect for science, shown in the large amounts of money it spent on the observatory. And she was amazed to learn that thousands of women were studying science in St. Petersburg. "How many thousand women . . . are studying science in the whole State of New York?" she wondered. "I doubt if there are five hundred." She was further impressed to learn that the Russian government had founded a medical school for women, unthought of in the United States.

The way the Russians practiced their religion impressed Maria, even though she didn't share their beliefs. In Russian churches, unlike American churches, there were as many men as women in the congregations.

"Then there is the *democracy* of the church . . . ," Maria wrote. "The oneness and equality before God are always recognized. A Russian gentleman, as he prays, does not look around, and move away from the poor beggar next to him."

When she talked with some young Russian women on a train, Maria discovered that they longed for a Russian women's college. But when Maria suggested that they could found one themselves, they answered, "We have not the energy of the American girl."

But Maria knew that in the United States, in spite of the success of "Vassar's folly," many people continued to doubt the capabilities of the "American girl." They still worried about whether the studies at a first-rate college were too burdensome for the female mind. At Vassar itself, there was much anxiety about the health of the students. If any of the girls became seriously ill, the enemies of the college would certainly blame the "unsuitable" academic standards.

Maria was exasperated by this nonsense, but she tried to keep her sense of humor. Once she had told the English astronomer John Herschel, "The examinations [at Vassar], Sir John, are *so* stiff that three young ladies died!" The Herschels thought this was funny too, and Maria's quip became a family joke.

The year that Maria traveled to Russia, she also attended the first meeting of the Social Science Association in Boston. There she heard President Charles Eliot of Harvard College say, "The minds of women are as different from men as are their bodies. . . . They cannot bear the stress of hard study." And mathematician Benjamin Peirce, the same man who had so highly recommended Maria for the position at Vassar, added that "it would be a pity if women became unlovely through too much education."

In the fall of 1873, Maria returned to Vassar more determined than ever to work for women's education. "I believe in women," she declared, "even more than I do in astronomy." With other fighters for women's rights, including Julia Ward Howe, Lucy Stone, and Mary Livermore, she helped plan a women's congress in New York City. Susan B. Anthony and Elizabeth Cady Stanton also took part. The goal of the congress was to form a group that would work for women's rights, and the congress was successful: the Association for the Advancement of Women was born.

In 1875, at the age of fifty-seven, Maria led the third annual Women's Congress, in Syracuse, as president of the AAW. During the next several years, she continued to work in the women's rights movement. Maria had no desire for the limelight, but she knew she had an important contribution to make to the cause, both because of who she was — one of the leading astronomers in the country — and because of what she had to say. As a speaker she was dignified, logical, and sensible, but she did not mince words. "Let no one suppose," she said pointedly, "that any woman in all the ages has had a fair chance in science."

❂   ❂   ❂

Meanwhile, there seemed to be more progress in astronomy than in women's rights. It was now possible, by studying the light given off by a star, to detect known chemical elements in that star. A technique had also been invented to measure how fast a star was moving toward or away from our solar system. As for Maria and her students, they continued to track comets. They took photographs of the planet Saturn, one of Maria's favorite subjects with its rings and moons. They also took daily photographs of the sun — Maria Mitchell was one of the first astronomers to do so.

In 1878 Maria led a group of women to Denver to observe the total solar eclipse. It was a journey of thousands of miles, as Maria noted, "for an observation which would last two minutes forty seconds." To Maria and her students, the trip was worth all the effort. Watching the moon's shadow race across the vast open landscape, the women felt "serious and reverent," experiencing the event as "a token of the inviolability of law."

CHAPTER 11

The Curtain That
Hides the Infinite

Maria Mitchell was now in her sixties, but her mind was no more "settled on religious subjects" than when she had left the Nantucket Meeting of the Society of Friends. After a lifetime of pursuing truth, her most urgent questions were still unanswered. She must have felt more than ever what she had expressed in her diary in 1854: "The world of learning is so broad, and the human soul is so limited in power! We reach forth and strain every nerve, but we seize only a bit of the curtain that hides the infinite from us."

There were times when she could almost see the Infinite through the nature of the cosmos. Contemplating the immense voids between the members of the solar system, she mused, "If God expresses infinite force by the mechanical powers at work in Nature, if he shows the infinite Artist in the wonderful beauty of nature, infinite wisdom in the creation of mind, what does he express by vacant spaces? Does he typify his own infinite loneliness?"

Maria continued to discuss religious questions with her friends and to listen intently to preachers. "If there were no future state of rewards and punishments," said one clergyman, speaking of heaven and hell, "it would be better to believe in one." Maria's incredulous response was, "Did he mean to say, 'Better to believe a lie'?"

One student who joined in the Sunday evening meetings of the "Rads" at the Vassar observatory remembered how angry Maria became at the theological proposition that human beings were basically bad. "When the conversation turned on the subject of total depravity she promptly pronounced the doctrine a most monstrous one, saying that she, for instance, never in her life [had] done anything that she knew was wrong, and therefore she could not but believe that evil was the result simply of poor judgment and mis-education."

Above all, Maria pursued the burning question, Is there life after death? It was a subject she discussed over and over with her friends, noting their answers thoughtfully. Joseph Henry at the Smithsonian Institution, ill and not far from the end of his life, told her that he had come to think of death as a friend. "I *cherish* the belief in immortality," he asserted; he even thought scientific evidence was on its side.

Professor Peirce at Harvard, the enthusiastic backer of Maria Mitchell but not of women in his classroom, also expected life after death. "I believe with St. Paul that there is a spiritual body," he told her. However, in

Maria's judgment, Peirce's conclusions were not always to be trusted. After reading his scientific paper entitled "Heat of the Sun," she commented, "I did not think it very sound."

When she visited another old friend, the poet John Greenleaf Whittier, Maria recorded that "his faith seems to be unbounded in the goodness of God, and his belief in moral accountability." As for whether there was life after death, Whittier thought the answer was too obvious for discussion. He simply stared at her. "The idea of Maria Mitchell's being snuffed out!"

Maria, like her mother, had been energetic and healthy all of her hard-working life. But in the fall of 1880 she became so ill that she was unable to teach most of the first term at Vassar. Mary Whitney, her assistant, took over until Maria was well enough to return to her classes.

However, the good health Maria had enjoyed up until now never quite returned. "I observed in the meridian room last night; working with telescopes always cheers me," wrote Maria in her diary in November of 1881. "I am hoping that the cramping of my hands means nothing — but it is new to me. I did not go to chapel today, but worked on a lesson."

Maria pushed herself to go on because there was always important work to be done. On any clear day or night, there was something worth watching in the skies. In 1882 she and her students photographed the transit of Venus across the sun, a rare astronomical event. There was the ongoing project of tracking and photographing sunspots; there were often comets and meteor showers to observe. And there were Jupiter and Saturn, Maria's favorite astronomical subjects, whenever these planets were in a favorable position to be observed.

One cold, clear day in 1885, Maria counted seconds for her students as they observed an annular eclipse of the sun. Her memory took her back to another perfectly cold, clear day, fifty-four years ago, when she had proudly counted seconds while her father manned the telescope. Just as William Mitchell had once shared his passion and knowledge with his twelve-year-old daughter, Maria Mitchell was now sharing her passion and knowledge with these young women, her daughters in spirit.

Frustrated by the continuing shortage of money for the observatory, Maria began her own fund-raising campaign. Benson Lossing, her good friend on the board of trustees, wrote her a note of praise in 1886: "There could be no more efficient 'beggar' for the Vassar Observatory, I think, than the honored and beloved Professor of Astronomy who inhabits it." This was probably true, but the "begging" took a great deal of Maria's time and energy.

Maria also continued to work for women's rights.

For several years she had served the Association for the Advancement of Women as chair of the committee on science, promoting the cause of science education. She attended meetings of various women's groups, including the New England Women's Club of Boston and the New York Sorosis. She gave lectures and challenged the backlash against the women's movement. "It wears upon me," she wrote, "when I hear women say, 'Men are no longer so ready to give up a seat in the cars [train], since the women's agitation arose.'" With characteristic quiet logic, she went on, "Is such a statement true? If true, is it of any consequence? Also — One grain of fair-dealing is worth more than a *bushel* of courtesy. "

Empty courtesy was not Maria's style, but she was known for her fairness and kindness. She regularly sent money to the aging Martha Bowles, who had helped nurse Lydia Mitchell in her last illness. As Maria wrote one of her students, "Probably you have cares and anxieties of your own; a little lift given to another will lighten your own burdens."

Maria's older brother, Andrew, had died in 1871, and her older sister, Sally Mitchell Barney, in 1876. But Maria's younger sisters and brothers — Anne, Frank, William Forster, Phebe, Henry, and Kate — were all still living. They knew she was overworking herself, and they tried to get her to slow down. Maria's goal was to continue teaching until she turned seventy, but by December of 1887 she was having trouble working algebra problems that once would have been simple for her. During Christmas vacation, she was ill again.

In January of 1888, Maria wrote to President James Monroe Taylor, announcing her resignation: "I had much hoped to continue until June, but my more than half century of work has worn me out." She advised that Mary Whitney, her assistant, be appointed the new Professor of Astronomy.

The college offered Maria a permanent home at Vassar, but she decided to move back to Lynn. There she would spend her retirement years with her sister Kate and her family. Knowing how important work was to her health and happiness, Maria built a small observatory, designed by her nephew William Kendall, who was an architect, in the backyard.

"I have put up my observatory at the opposite shore of America and the other extreme, in size, with Lick," she wrote her colleague Dr. Avery, referring to the mighty Lick Observatory that had just opened in California. Maria sent friends copies of a photograph of herself outside her little observatory. There was a poignant contrast between this picture and the portrait painted by Hermione Dassel back in 1851. That portrait had shown an eager, intent young astronomer; in this photo Maria sat passively, with her hat on her lap and a shawl over the back of the chair.

In retirement, Maria also launched into the project of learning Greek, one of the few subjects she had not mastered at the Nantucket Atheneum long ago. "It will take 30 years," she joked to a friend, "but I may find chances for it, in the other world. Maria Dame [Kate's daughter] is my teacher."

However, Maria's hopes of continuing to work in retirement didn't last long. When a serious fall ended her daily walks, her health failed further. In October of 1888, she wrote one of her last letters, to President Taylor at Vassar. "Good health and good times to you all," she said; "the world is better while Vassar lives, because it is in it."

Even during her final illness, Maria kept her sense of humor. One day toward the end, when Maria was bedridden and hardly able to speak, her sister Phebe greeted her, "Thee looks well this morning, Maria." That must have struck Maria — who knew she had never been a beauty and couldn't possibly look well now — as funny. A nursery rhyme about a fortune-seeking gentleman and a pretty milkmaid — a rhyme Maria had probably chanted to Phebe years ago, when they were growing up on Nantucket — popped into her head. Maria started to croak out a line of the rhyme: "My face is my fortune — " Phebe, getting the joke, finished the line: " — sir, she said."

As Maria was lying in bed, perhaps she remembered the farewell lines she had written for her first graduating astronomy students:

Willing to bear the parting and pain,
Believing we all shall meet again;

That if God is God and truth is truth,
We shall meet again and all in youth.

Surely Maria recited to herself, during those months of
illness, her favorite poem, "The spacious firmament on
high." Perhaps in her mind's eye the entire solar system
revolved to the stately rhythm of the words:

In reason's ear they all rejoice,
And utter forth a glorious voice;
Forever singing as they shine,
"The hand that made us is divine."

Maria Mitchell died on June 28, 1889. She was
buried on Nantucket, in the Prospect Hill Cemetery,
which is now in the shadow of the new Loines Observatory. At her funeral, President Taylor spoke: "It would
be vain for me to try to tell just what it was in Miss
Mitchell that attracted us who loved her. It was this
combination of great strength and independence, of
deep affection and tenderness, breathed through and
through with the sentiment of a perfectly genuine
life. . . . Professor Mitchell has always been seeking the
truth and I think she has found it now."

❊　　❊　　❊

When Maria Mitchell was a young girl growing up on
Nantucket, she studied by the light of a whale-oil lamp,

and the steamboat was a newer invention to the Mitchells than spacecraft are to us today. Before Maria retired from Vassar, she was using some electric lights (probably battery-powered) in the observatory, and the gasoline-powered automobile was being developed.

Changes just as momentous had taken place in society. In the 1830s, the only college that admitted women was co-educational Oberlin College in Ohio. By the 1870s, there were several fine women's colleges besides Vassar, and many co-educational colleges and universities around the country.

Maria Mitchell herself had had something to do with this change. From the time she burst into the national consciousness as the discoverer of Comet 1847 VI, she had been a model of what a woman, given the chance, could accomplish in science. Those who claimed that a woman's brain would collapse under the strain of studying mathematics and science had been refuted by the very existence of Maria Mitchell.

But Maria Mitchell had done far more than exist. She had resolved to give up the life of an independent scientist and devote her efforts "to the intellectual culture of women." In her work with young women at Vassar and in her struggle to promote the cause of women's education, she had demonstrated how much she meant what she had stated: "I believe in women more than I even do in astronomy."

Maria Mitchell was given many awards and honors during her lifetime. She was the first woman admitted to the American Academy of Arts and Sciences, to the American Association for the Advancement of Science, and to the American Philosophical Society (founded by her distant relative Benjamin Franklin). She received honorary degrees, including one from Columbia College. A crater on the moon was named after her.

After her death, Maria was given still more honors. A tablet inscribed with her name was put in the New York University Hall of Fame; her name was carved on a frieze over the front of the Boston Public Library. In 1994, she was inducted into the National Women's Hall of Fame in Seneca Falls, New York. But even had she known of these later honors, her greatest satisfaction would still have been the effect she had on the lives of her students.

The way the young women at Vassar felt about Maria Mitchell is perhaps best indicated by the song they always sang at her Dome Parties. The last verse goes like this:

> Sing her praises, sing her praises,
>   good woman that she is,
> For to give us joy and welcome her
>   chiefest pleasure 'tis,
> Let her name be sung forever,
>   till through space her praises whiz,
> Good woman that she is.

Unmusical Maria probably didn't appreciate the quality of her students' light, clear voices when they sang that song. But she loved their high spirits, deep affection, and delightful touch of silliness.

Mary Whitney did follow Maria as Professor of Astronomy at Vassar. And many of Maria's other students went on to become scientists or mathematicians or educators. But even those who did not follow in her footsteps had been deeply affected by her. They remembered her silver curls and humorous mouth, the penetrating but kind gaze of her dark eyes. They remembered her words: "I cannot expect to make you astronomers, but I do expect that you will invigorate your minds by the effort at healthy modes of thinking. . . . When we are chafed and fretted by small cares, a look at the stars will show us the littleness of our own interests." And "A small apparatus well used will do wonders. . . . Newton rolled up the cover of a book; he put a small glass at one end, and a large brain at the other — it was enough."

"If it were only possible to tell you of what Professor Mitchell did for one of her girls!" wrote a student. "'Her girls!' It meant so much to come into daily contact with such a woman! There is no need of speaking of her ability; the world knows what that was. But as her class-room was unique, having something of home in its belongings, so its atmosphere differed from that of all others. Anxiety and nervous strain were left outside of the door."

This was especially remarkable in light of the high standards Maria held for her students. "Whatever apology other women may have for loose, ill-finished work," she told them, "or work not finished at all, you will have none."

As for Maria Mitchell herself, she needed no apologies. She had worked hard and well. She had finished her work. She was, as President John Raymond of Vassar had called her, a "bright, unwavering star." And John Greenleaf Whittier was right — Maria Mitchell could not be snuffed out.

My Sources for This Book

In writing this book, I drew on a number of valuable sources. The principal source was Phebe Mitchell Kendall's *Maria Mitchell: Life, Letters, and Journals,* published in 1896 by Lee and Shephard. Also important were papers from the archives of the Nantucket Maria Mitchell Association and the Nantucket Historical Society in Nantucket, Massachusetts; and papers from the archives of the Vassar College Library Special Collections Department, Poughkeepsie, New York. Other sources include Cornelia Raymond's *Memories of a Child of Vassar* (Poughkeepsie, N.Y.: Vassar College, 1940); Frances A. Wood's *Earliest Days at Vassar* (Poughkeepsie, N.Y.: Vassar College Press, 1909); and Helen Wright's *Sweeper in the Sky: The Life of Maria Mitchell* (New York: Macmillan, 1949).

I am deeply indebted to Henry Albers, Professor Emeritus of Astronomy, Vassar College; to Janet Coryell, Associate Professor of History at Western Michigan University; and to Elizabeth Daniels, College Historian and Professor of English at Vassar College. They not only generously shared information related to Maria Mitchell but also read the manuscript of this book and gave helpful suggestions for revision.

Suggestions for Further Reading

Asimov, Isaac. *Eyes on the Universe: A History of the Telescope.* Boston: Houghton Mifflin, 1975.

Gives a clear overview of the development of astronomy through different periods in history. Includes photos and diagrams of different types of telescopes.

Chapman, Robert D., and Brandt, John C. *The Comet Book: A Guide for the Return of Halley's Comet.* Boston: Jones and Bartlett Publishers, Inc., 1984.

All you ever wanted to know about comets, and more.

Philbrick, Nathaniel. *Away Off Shore: Nantucket Island and Its People, 1602-1890.* Nantucket: Mill Hill Press, 1994.

Includes sections on the Nantucket Quakers, the Nantucket whaling industry, and Maria Mitchell.

Richardson, Robert S. *The Star Lovers*. New York: Macmillan, 1967.

The lives of selected famous astronomers, from the sixteenth to the mid-twentieth century.

Sullivan, George. *The Day the Women Got the Vote: A Photo History of the Women's Movement*. New York: Scholastic, Inc., 1994.

A concise overview of the women's movement, from the late eighteenth to the late twentieth century. Lots of illustrations.

West, Jessamyn, ed. *The Quaker Reader*. New York: Viking, 1962.

Selections from writings by members of the Society of Friends, from the seventeenth through the mid-twentieth century. Unfortunately, this book includes nothing by Nantucket Quakers, but it does include a vivid description of silent meeting as the Quakers experienced it, and some anti-slavery writings by Quakers.

Wright, Helen. *Sweeper in the Sky: The Life of Maria Mitchell*. New York: Macmillan, 1949.

A thorough and readable but highly dramatized biography of Maria Mitchell. It's not always easy to tell where actual fact ends and the author's imagination takes over.

Acknowledgments

The author and publisher gratefully acknowledge permission to quote material from the following sources:

Excerpts from the papers in the Maria Mitchell Collection, courtesy of the Nantucket Maria Mitchell Association. Any errors in interpretation or reproduction of the quotations are the responsibility of the author and not the Nantucket Maria Mitchell Association.

Excerpts from two of Maria Mitchell's letters, courtesy of the Nantucket Historical Association.

Brief excerpts, amounting to approximately 1,000 words, from the Maria Mitchell Papers, courtesy of Special Collections of Vassar College Libraries.

Index